WHAT IS LIVING AND WHAT IS DEAD
OF THE PHILOSOPHY OF HEGEL

WHAT IS LIVING AND WHAT IS DEAD OF THE PHILOSOPHY OF HEGEL

BY

BENEDETTO CROCE

TRANSLATED FROM THE ORIGINAL TEXT OF
THE THIRD ITALIAN EDITION, 1912

BY

DOUGLAS AINSLIE
B.A. (Oxon.), M.R.A.S.

NEW YORK / RUSSELL & RUSSELL

FIRST PUBLISHED IN 1915
REISSUED, 1969, BY RUSSELL & RUSSELL
A DIVISION OF ATHENEUM PUBLISHERS, INC.
BY ARRANGEMENT WITH MACMILLAN & CO. LTD., LONDON
L. C. CATALOG CARD NO: 79-83845
PRINTED IN THE UNITED STATES OF AMERICA

TRANSLATOR'S NOTE

READERS of this translation will observe that I have followed the Italian in discarding where the original does so the use of capitals for the words idea, spirit and so forth. It is true that they are printed with capitals in German ; but then, so are all other substantives, and by avoiding their use, such words as idea and spirit are better understood as immanent rather than as transcendental "things-in-themselves."

I used "gnoseology" in my translation of the *Philosophy of the Practical* instead of the paraphrase "theory of knowledge." This word, regularly formed from the Greek, seems to me worthy a place in English, which has made no difficulty about accepting an analogous, but not identical, term such as Epistemology. When neologisms cover a new thought or facilitate, by abbreviating, expression, it seems to me that they are always legitimate, and I have not hesitated to introduce one or two other words thus employed. The tendency to avoid neologism at all costs by the adoption of paraphrase, frequent in contemporary English writers, seems to me to frustrate the very purpose which it is intended to serve, rendering yet more difficult by the very commonness of the words used as paraphrase the already sufficiently subtle qualifications of philosophy.

AUTHOR'S NOTE

THE study, *What is living and what is dead of the Philosophy of Hegel*, was published in 1906 (Bari, Laterza), and contained an essay on Hegelian bibliography as an appendix. This has since been increased in the German and French translations of that volume and would now have need of not a few additions. But it has seemed to me opportune in the present [1] collection to suppress altogether the bibliographical portion as something extraneous to its nature, and to republish it, if ever, separately. And indeed, if any one will give himself the trouble of looking through, correcting, completing and keeping it up to date for the use of students of Hegel, I propose

[1] The Essay on Hegel is the first of a series of essays upon philosophical subjects contained in the volume from which this essay has been selected for translation into English.—D. A.

vii

to present him with that first study of mine, with permission to exercise upon it most fully the *jus utendi et abutendi.* In this reimpression of the critical study of 1906 will be found instead certain elucidations of various points of the Hegelian philosophy, which answer to censures and objections that have been made to me; though I have as a rule preferred, as more persuasive, objective treatment or retreatment of disputed points to polemic properly so called.

B. CROCE.

RAIANO (AQUILA),
September 1912.

CONTENTS

PAGE

I. THE DIALECTIC OR SYNTHESIS OF OPPOSITES .   I

II. EXPLANATIONS RELATING TO THE HISTORY OF THE DIALECTIC 33

III. THE DIALECTIC AND THE CONCEPTION OF REALITY 52

IV. THE NEXUS OF THE DISTINCTS AND THE FALSE APPLICATION OF THE DIALECTIC FORM . . 78

V. THE METAMORPHOSIS OF ERRORS INTO PARTICULAR CONCEPTS AND DEGREES OF TRUTH (STRUCTURE OF THE LOGIC) 100

VI. THE METAMORPHOSIS OF PARTICULAR CONCEPTS INTO PHILOSOPHICAL ERRORS . . . 120
     I. Art and Language (Æsthetic).

VII. THE METAMORPHOSIS OF PARTICULAR CONCEPTS INTO PHILOSOPHICAL ERRORS . . . 134
     II. History (Idea of a Philosophy of History).

VIII. THE METAMORPHOSIS OF PARTICULAR CONCEPTS INTO PHILOSOPHICAL ERRORS . . . 150
     III. Nature (Idea of a Philosophy of Nature).

ix

PAGE

IX. The Construction of the False Sciences
and the Application of the Dialectic to
the Individual and to the Empirical   .   174

X. Dualism not overcome   192

XI. The Criticism and Continuation of the
Thought of Hegel   203
Conclusion.

TRANSLATOR'S INTRODUCTION [1]

THE following lines were written before the outbreak of war, but I see no reason to qualify any of the statements therein contained. The madness and immoralism of twentieth century Germany has nothing in common with her great writers of a hundred years ago and more. There has been a great decline of German thought coincident with material prosperity and aspiration for universal dominion.

Readers of the following pages, accustomed to Hegel's Himalayan severity and ruggedness of style and to the arid and difficult treatment of the Hegelian philosophy, so long in vogue, both here and in Germany, will probably be surprised at the profound yet pellucid clarity of Croce's thought. Hegel has at last found a critic and interpreter equal to the task, in the thinker who has already given us complete the *Philosophy of the Spirit*. Croce has passed beyond and therefore been able

[1] Some of these thoughts are taken from other essays of Croce.

to look back upon Hegel, to unravel the gorgeous yet tangled skein of his system, and supply to all future students the clue of Ariadne.

Who but Croce would have thought of recommending that Hegel should be read like a poet? Were it not for his own work upon æsthetic, such a statement would seem absurd; but in the light of the two degrees of theoretic knowledge and of the formation of logic from æsthetic intuitions, such a remark assumes its full significance. Rather, then, than dwell for ever upon some technical difficulty, such as that presented by the first triad of the Logic, he recommends us to read Hegel "like a poet," that is without paying undue attention to the verbal form, the historical accident of what he says, but full attention to its poetic truth.   In reading a philosopher, we should seek his inspiration in the mazes of his text, without paying undue attention to the pedantries and formulæ with which such a writer as Hegel is (historically) overlaid. We should see in the Hegelian triads the mighty effort of the philosopher against Eleaticism and all forms of Nihilism, and his attempt to create a new and superior form of Heracliticism. The cut-and-dried Hegel of the schools is thus to be avoided; and when with Croce's help we have scraped the lichen of his formulae from the thought of Hegel, we find beneath it the true philosopher, the hater of all that is abstract and motionless, of the should-be that never is, of the ideal that is not real.

The title of this book sufficiently explains its scope and object. The magnificent critique and explanation of the dialectic is followed by the exposition of one of Hegel's two great errors, the confusion of distincts and opposites, and of its far-reaching evil consequences for a great part of the Hegelian system. That this error should appear in the Logic itself is characteristic of Hegel, who is not guilty of any mere inadvertence or blunder, but errs grandly in a vital part of his system. One of the most important deductions from this error is that of the death of art, to be merged, according to Hegel, in philosophy. Croce's refutation of this fallacy and of the application of the dialectic to the empirical world, were they his sole contribution to philosophic criticism and research, would suffice to lay all students of Hegel beneath an obligation of enlightened gratitude to the philosopher of Naples.

Croce points out how it was owing to the application of the dialectic of opposites to the category of distincts that Hegel conceived so great a contempt for the practical as compared with the

theoretic world.   He was led by his theory to look
upon the former as one from which the thinker
freed himself by the power of his thought.   In
Hegel, the poet and the sage look down from
their tower of ivory upon the throng below.   He
conceived the dialectic as a temporal becoming,
a *progressus ad finitum*, and once he had attained
to the contemplative life, the sage would naturally
no longer desire any sort of intercourse with the
throng.   There would thus be cessation of the
dialectic.   But becoming cannot negate itself.
The true becoming is ideal ; it is the intelligence
of real becoming, in the same way as the universal
is not divergent or indifferent in respect to the
particular, but is the intelligence of the particular ;
so that universal and particular, ideal and real becoming, are the same.   Outside ideal becoming
is not real becoming, but only temporal becoming,
that is to say, arithmetical time, a construction of
the abstract intellect ; just as the real individual is
not outside the universal, but only the empirical individual, isolated, atomicized, monadized.   Eternity
and real time coincide, because the eternal is in
every instant and every instant is in the eternal.

Hegel's identification of the real and the
rational led him to support energetically the
action of the State and of all great men, and

his confusion of the ethical with the economic
led to the creation of Nietzsche's Superman, a
being above the morality of the throng. The
rationality of the real should, however, be closely
connected with the most rigid condemnation of
error and of evil, and the perpetuity of the dialectic
with the constancy of the true. The idea of finite
progress must therefore be looked upon as incomplete, until it has been enriched by the dialectic
with the idea of infinite progress. This latter,
taken by itself, is also void of content, for an
eternal approximation and never attaining is not
progress : it does not matter to Tantalus if the
sweet spring-water be a mile or an inch from his
lips, if he is never to touch it with them. The
symbol of humanity is neither God nor man, but
the God-man, Christ, Who is the eternal in the
temporal and the temporal in the eternal.
Another way of stating the same thing is to com-
bine the western idea of a perpetual breathless
pursuit of truth, and the static oriental idea of the
perpetual return. The spirit and history are
identical, as in their turn are philosophy and
history, because neither is complete without the
others. We possess the truth at every moment,
by the act of thinking, and this truth is at every
instant changed into will and nature, and therefore

into a new problem, which must be constantly added to, if it is to remain truth. A man may sacrifice all he has for the truth, even his own soul, but he can never sacrifice morality, owing to the contradiction that this would imply. Croce has more than a good word to say of the study of Hegel in Great Britain, and indeed he recently observed to the present writer that his own thought remained far more itself in the English than in the German versions of his *Æsthetic* and *Philosophy of the Practical*: in the latter it seemed to melt away. But the study of Hegel should receive a new and vigorous impetus from this work, which should do much to correct the widespread con-fusion of the data of empirical or natural science with true science, which is philosophy, the science of sciences. Philosophy assigns its sphere to each of the empirical sciences, and in their sphere philo-sophy is not competent. Confusion has arisen from the attempts so often made by natural scientists to solve problems outside their com-petency. A man may be an excellent entomo-logist, but his views upon the problem of know-ledge will be devoid of interest, unless he be also a philosopher. The domination of empiricism in this country has led to suspicion of thought which is simply thought as yet untranslated into volitional act. Discussing recently in London the origins of socialism with a leading statesman, he remárked to me that socialism was the result of modern economic conditions, factories, etc. He seemed disinclined to admit that socialism in its theoretic form first existed in the mind of Hegel and then filtered down through Feuerbach and Marx, to Sorel and the syndicalists of our day. There seems to exist the belief that thought can arise from psychical friction, like a spark from tinder. Reality is looked upon by many as the physical, mind as an epiphenomenon. Without the philosophers above mentioned, there could have been no "social question" as it presents itself to-day. The labour troubles of Roman days were settled more easily than those of the modern world because without the modern theoretic basis. They could not, however, have existed without some theoretic basis, however rudimentary. The French Revolution broke out first in the brain of Jean-Jacques Rousseau.

Much will, in my opinion, have been achieved by the publication in English of this book, if it lead our men of action—and as a nation the English have the genius of practical action—to respect Hegel as one of the greatest *practical* forces the world has ever seen. They are not likely to become mere dreamers by so doing, for here we run no risk of underrating those elements of empirical thought represented by aeroplanes and other automobiles. Matter changes place with far greater rapidity than heretofore, but there is one thing that is "never in a hurry," yet supremely worthy of attention, and that, as readers of Hegel know, is the idea.

DOUGLAS AINSLIE.

THE ATHENÆUM,
PALL MALL, LONDON.

WHAT IS LIVING AND WHAT IS DEAD
OF THE PHILOSOPHY OF HEGEL

I

THE DIALECTIC OR SYNTHESIS
OF OPPOSITES

HEGEL is one of those philosophers who have
made not only immediate reality but philosophy
itself the object of their thought, thus contribut-
ing to elaborate a *logic of philosophy*. I believe,
therefore, that the logic of philosophy (with the
consequences ensuing from it for the solution of
particular problems and for the conception of life)
was the goal to which the main effort of his mind
was directed. It was there that he found or
brought to perfection and full value, principles of
high importance which had been unknown to or
hardly mentioned by previous philosophers, or
insufficiently marked by them, and which may
therefore be considered as his true discoveries.

Strange is the aversion to this conception of a
logic of philosophy (for it is really very simple
and should be accepted as irresistibly evident).

It is the idea, in other words, that philosophy
proceeds by a method peculiar to itself, the theory
of which should be sought and formulated. No
one doubts that mathematics has a method of its
own, which is studied in the logic of mathematics ;
that the natural sciences have their method,
from which arises the logic of observation, of
experiment, of abstraction ; that historiography
has its method, and that therefore there is a
logic of the historical method ; that poetry and
art in general give us the logic of poetry and art,
i.e. æsthetic ; that in economic activity is inherent
a method, which is afterwards reflected in
economic science ; and that finally the moral
activity has its method, which is reflected in
ethic (or logic of the will, as it has sometimes
been called). But when we come to philosophy,
very many recoil from this conclusion : that it,
too, from the moment of its inception, must have
a method of its own, which must be determined.
Conversely, very few are surprised at the fact
that treatises on logic, while giving much space
to the consideration of the disciplines of the
mathematical and natural sciences, as a rule
give no special attention to the discipline of
philosophy, and often pass it over altogether in
silence.

It is very natural that a logic of philosophy should be denied by those who, owing to lack of reflection or mental confusion or eccentricity, deny philosophy in general. For it cannot be claimed that the theory of an object should be recognized when the reality of the object itself is denied. If philosophy does not exist, then the logic of philosophy does not exist. Good-bye to both; enjoy such a position if it satisfy you. But if I have called this spectacle strange, it is because we too often see those very philosophers or philosophizers, as the case may be, showing themselves altogether devoid of the conscious-ness of this inevitable necessity. Some of them assert that philosophy must follow the abstract-deductive method of mathematics. Others see for it no other way of salvation than a rigorous adherence to the experimental method. They dream and extol a philosophy studied in the laboratory and the clinic, an empirical metaphysic, and so on. Finally (and this is the latest fashion, which, if not new, is at least newly revived), we are now commended to an individual and fantastic philosophy, which produces itself like art. Thus, from the compasses to the bistouri, and from that to the zither! every method seems good for philosophy, save the method of philosophy itself.

One single observation should suffice against such views : namely, that if philosophy is to provide the understanding, and be as it were the reflective consciousness of art and history, of mathematics and of the researches of natural science, of the practical and moral activity, we fail to see how it can do this by conforming to the method of one of those particular objects. He who, when studying a poem, limits his study to the application of the poetical method, will feel in himself the creation of the poet, this or that particular work of art ; but he will not thus attain to a philosophic knowledge of the poem. He who limits himself to mathematical thinking, when studying a mathematical theory, will be the disciple, the critic, the perfecter of that theory ; but he will not attain knowledge of the nature of mathematical activity.   If the object of philosophy be not the production or the reproduction of art and mathematics and of the various other activities of man, but the comprehension (the understanding) of them all, this comprehension is itself an activity, proceeding by a method of its own, infused or implicit, which it is important to make explicit.

In any case the hope of understanding and of judging the work of Hegel is vain, if we do not always keep clearly before the mind that this problem which we have just enunciated was his main and principal problem, the central problem of the *Phenomenology of Spirit*, and of the new forms assumed by this book in the *Science of Logic* and in the *Encyclopaedia of Philosophical Sciences*. Almost all histories of philosophy, and even the special-monographs concerning Hegel (for example, the recent and most ample monograph by Kuno Fischer), consist in a summary repetition of the contents of his books, so close as to repeat his divisions by sections and chapters. But a complete exposition of Hegel's thought, an inward and critical exposition, should, in the first place and in chief part, be devoted to his doctrine of the nature of philosophic enquiry, and to the differences between such enquiry and other theoretic and non-theoretic forms.

Above all, what should be made clear is the triple character that philosophic thought assumes in Hegel, in relation to the three spiritual modes or attitudes with which it is most readily confused. Philosophic thought is for Hegel: firstly, concept; secondly, universal; thirdly, concrete. It is *concept*, that is to say it is not feeling, or rapture, or intuition, or any other

similar alogical psychical state, incapable of exact
demonstration.   This distinguishes philosophy
from theories of mysticism and of immediate
knowledge ; for these have at the most a negative
significance, in so far as they recognize that
philosophy cannot be constructed by the method
of the empirical and natural sciences, *i.e.* of the
sciences of the finite.   They are, if you will,
profound, but with an "empty profundity."
Hegel becomes ferociously satirical against
mysticism, with its frenzies, its sighings, its raising
the eyes to heaven, its bowing the neck and
clasping the hands, its faintings, its prophetic
accents, its mysterious phrases of the initiates.
He always maintains that philosophy should have
a rational and intelligible form ; that it should be,
"not esoteric but exoteric," not a thing of sects,
but of humanity.   The philosophic concept is
universal, not merely general.   It is not to be
confounded with general representations, as for
instance, "house," "horse," "blue," which are
usually termed concepts, owing to a custom
which Hegel calls barbaric.   This establishes the
difference between philosophy and the empirical
or natural sciences, which are satisfied with types
and class-conceptions.   Finally, the philosophic
universal is *concrete*: it is not the making of a

skeleton of reality, but the comprehension of it in its fulness and richness. Philosophic abstractions are not arbitrary but necessary, and are therefore adequate to the real, which they do not mutilate or falsify. And this establishes the difference between philosophy and the mathematical disciplines; for these latter do not justify their points of departure, but "command them," and we must, says Hegel, obey the command to draw such and such lines, in the belief that this will be "opportune" for the conduct of the demonstration. Philosophy, on the other hand, has for its object that which really is; and it must completely justify itself, without admitting or allowing any presupposition.[1]

And in order to elucidate this triple difference, according to which the true concept, *i.e.* the philosophical concept, shows itself logical, universal, and concrete, it would be necessary to include in a complete exposition the minor doctrines, which are attached to the first and fundamental doctrine, some of which are of great importance, such as the resumption of the ontological argument (the defence of Saint Anselm against Kant), which maintains that in the

---

[1] See especially the introduction to the *Phenomenology* and the preliminaries to the *Encyclopaedia*.

philosophic concept, as distinct and different from mere representations of particulars, essence implies existence. Another is the review of the doctrine which regards the "judgment" as a connexion of subject and predicate. That doctrine is based on something that is not clearly intelligible to thought, and is therefore inadequate to philosophy, of which the true form is the "syllogism," in so far as that has the logical character of reuniting itself with itself; others, again, are the critique of the theory, which considers the concept to be a compound of "marks" (which Hegel calls the true "mark" of the superficiality of ordinary logic); the critique of divisions into species and classes; the demonstration (which may have curative efficacy in our times) of the vanity of every "logical calculus"; and not a few others besides.

But it is not my intention to offer in these pages a complete exposition of Hegel's system, nor even of his logical doctrine; but rather to concentrate all attention upon the most characteristic part of his thought, upon the new aspects of truth revealed by him, and upon the errors which he allowed to persist or in which he became entangled. For this reason, then, I set aside the various theses briefly mentioned above (from which it seems to me impossible to dissent, although I recognize too how necessary it is that they should be studied, since they form the often neglected A B C of philosophy), and I come without further ado to the point around which all the disputes have been kindled and against which his opponents have aimed their direct denials— the treatment of the problem of *opposites*.

This is a problem whose terms must be clearly defined if we wish to understand its gravity and difficulty. The philosophic concept (which, as has been mentioned, is a concrete universal), in so far as it is concrete, does not exclude distinctions, indeed it includes them in itself. It is the universal, distinct in itself, re- sulting from those distinctions. As empirical concepts are distinguished into classes and sub- classes, so the philosophic concept possesses its particular forms, of which it is not the mechanical aggregate, but the organic whole, in which every form unites itself intimately with the others and with the whole. For example, fancy and intellect, in relation to the concept of spirit or spiritual activity, are particular philosophic concepts ; but they are not outside or beneath spirit, they are indeed spirit itself in those particular forms ; nor is the one separated from the other, like two

entities each confined to itself, and external to
the other, but the one passes into the other.
Hence fancy, as is commonly said, however
distinct it may be from intellect, is the foundation
of intellect and indispensable to it.

Our thought however, in investigating reality,
finds itself face to face, not only with *distinct*, but
also with *opposed* concepts. These latter cannot
be identified with the former without more ado,
nor be considered as special cases of them, as if
they were a sort of distinct concepts. The logical
category of distinction is one thing, and the
category of opposition is another. As has been
said, two distinct concepts unite with one another,
although they are distinct ; but two opposite concepts seem to exclude one another. Where one
enters, the other totally disappears. A distinct
concept is presupposed by and lives in its other,
which follows it in the sequence of ideas. An
opposite concept is slain by its opposite : the
saying, *mors tua vita mea* applies here. Examples
of distinct concepts are those already mentioned,
of fancy and intellect. And to these others
could be added, such as rights, morality and the
like. But examples of opposite concepts are
drawn from those numerous couples of words, of
which our language is full and which certainly

do not constitute peaceable and friendly couples. Such are the antitheses of *true* and *false*, of *good* and *evil*, *beautiful* and *ugly*, *value* and *lack of value*, *joy* and *sorrow*, *activity* and *passivity*, *positive* and *negative*, *life* and *death*, *being* and *not-being*, and so on. It is impossible to confuse the two series, distincts and opposites: so conspicuously do they differ.

Now, if distinction do not impede, if indeed it rather render possible the concrete unity of the philosophic concept, it does not seem possible that the same should be true of opposition. Opposition gives rise to deep fissures in the bosom of the philosophic universal and of each of its particular forms, and to irreconcilable dualisms. Instead of finding the concrete universal, the organic whole of reality which it seeks, thought seems everywhere to run against two universals, opposing and menacing each other. In this way, the fulfilment of philosophy is impeded; and since an activity which cannot attain to its fulfilment, thereby shows that it has imposed an absurd task on itself, philosophy itself, the whole of philosophy, is menaced with failure.

The seriousness of this impasse is the reason that the human mind has always laboured at this problem of opposites, without, however, always

clearly realizing what it has been doing. And
one of the solutions upon which it has relied in
the course of centuries, has consisted in excluding
opposition from the philosophic concept, and in
maintaining the unreality of that perilous logical
category.   The facts, to tell the truth, proved just
the opposite ; but the facts were denied and only
one of the terms was accepted, the other being
declared " illusion " ; or, what comes to the same
thing, a merely quantitative difference was drawn
between the two.   This logical doctrine of
opposites is contained in the philosophic systems
of sensationalism, of empiricism, of materialism,
of mechanism, or however otherwise they may
be termed.   Thought and truth appeared in
them in turn, a secretion of the brain, or an
effect of habit and association ; virtue, a mirage
of egoism ;   beauty, a refinement of sensuality ;
the ideal, some kind of voluptuous or capricious
dream ; and so on.

Another logical doctrine, which posits opposition as a fundamental category, has for
centuries employed its force against this first
doctrine.   It is found in the various dualistic
systems, which reassert the antithesis that the
first, with a delicate sleight of hand, had caused
to disappear.   These systems accentuate both

terms, being and not-being, good and evil, true and false, ideal and real, those of the one series being at variance with those of the other. Without doubt, the dualistic view retains its value against abstract monism : a polemical value due to its denial of the other's negation. But in itself, it is as little satisfactory as the other, because if the first sacrifices opposition to unity, the second sacrifices unity to opposition.

In thought both these sacrifices are so impossible, that we continually see those who maintain the one doctrine turning more or less consciously into maintainers of the other. The unitarians surreptitiously introduce the duality of opposites, under the guise of the duality of reality and of illusion : an illusion with which they could no more dispense than with reality itself, so that they sometimes even say that the spring of life is in illusion. And the opposition-ists all admit some sort of identity or unity of opposites unattainable by the human mind, owing to its imperfection, but necessary in order adequately to think reality. In this way, both become involved in contradictions, and come to recognize that they have not solved the problem which they had set themselves, and that it still remains a problem.

For "necessary illusion," or "necessary imperfection of the human mind," are mere words, to which, try as we will, we cannot give any meaning. We know only accidental and relative illusions, individual and relative imperfections. A reality other than the real, a mind beyond the human mind, we can neither conceive nor constitute a term in any comparison. Thus reality and mind show us both unity and opposition. And (as Leibniz said of philosophical systems) the unitarians, in so far as they affirm the first, the oppositionists, in so far as they affirm the second, are right in what they affirm and wrong in what they deny. Hegel is never weary of admiring the virile firmness of the materialists and sensationalists and monists of every sort in asserting the unity of the real, and if, owing to the historical conditions in which his thought developed, he admired the dualistic forms less, and indeed never lost an opportunity of expressing his antipathy to them, on the other hand he never forgot that the consciousness of opposition is equally invincible and equally justifiable with that of unity.

The case, then, seems desperate; and no less desperate is the case of desperation. For, to

declare the question insoluble would itself compel
us to consider, whether, by that very declaration,
we had not already cut the knot in favour of
thought, that is to say, of hope.   The casual
observer of the history of philosophy sees a
restoration of dualism follow every affirmation
of monism, and vice versa : each unable wholly
to strangle the other, but able to hold it in check
for a time.   It would seem almost as though, when
man has satiated himself with the uniformity of
monism, he distracts himself with the variety of
dualism ; and, when he is tired of this, he plunges
again into monism, and alternates the two move-
ments, thus tempering hygienically the one
with the other.   The casual observer, at every
epidemic of materialism, says with a smile, Wait ;
now will come spiritualism.   And when spiritualism celebrates its chiefest triumphs, he smiles in
the same way and says, Wait ; materialism will
return in a little while !   But the smile is forced,
or soon vanishes, for there is nothing really
cheerful in the condition of him who is ceaselessly
tossed from one extreme to another, as by an
invincible force beyond control.

Nevertheless, amid the difficulties which I have
made clear, there is at the bottom of our souls
a secret conviction, that this unconquerable

dualism, this insoluble dilemma, is ultimately conquerable and soluble : that the idea of unity is not irreconcilable with that of opposition, and that we can and should think opposition in the form of a concept, which is supreme unity. Ingenuous thought (which is usually called non-philosophical, but would perhaps be better called naïvely, or potentially, philosophical) is not embarrassed at the difficulty : it thinks at once both unity and opposition. Its motto is not *mors tua vita mea*, but *concordia discors*. It recognises that life is a struggle, but nevertheless a harmony ; that virtue is a combat against ourselves, but that it is nevertheless ourselves. It recognizes that, when one opposition has been overcome, a new opposition springs from the very bosom of the unity, so there must be a new conquest, then a new opposition, and so on ; but it recognizes, too, that this is just the way of life. It knows nothing of exclusive systems : the wisdom of proverbs gives one blow to the hoop and another to the barrel, and gives advice now with optimistic, now with pessimistic observations, which deny and complete one another in turn. What is wanting to ingenuous thought, to potential philosophy ? Implicitly, nothing. And so, amidst the smoke and the dust

of the battles of science, we always sigh for the
good sense, for the truth which each one can
find immediately in himself, without recourse to
the labourings, the subtleties, and the exaggera-
tions of professional philosophers. But the sigh
is vain! the battle has been joined, and there is
no way to peace save through victory. Ingenuous
thought (and this is its defect) cannot give the
grounds of its affirmations: it vacillates before
every objection; it becomes confused and contra-
dicts itself. Its truths are not complete truths,
because they are not found united, but merely
placed alongside one another. It works only
with juxtaposition, and fails in systematic
coherence. Contradictions and doubts and the
painful consciousness of antitheses are welcome;
welcome is all conflict if through it we are to
attain to the truth that is complete and secure
in itself. Such truth, indeed, though it differs
widely from the truth of ordinary and ingenuous
thought in degree of elaboration, cannot but be
substantially the same; and it is certainly a bad
sign when a philosophy is at variance with ingenuous consciousness. For this very reason it
often happens that when people meet a simple
and conclusive statement of philosophic truths,
that may have cost the labours of centuries, they

will shrug their shoulders and remark that the boasted discovery is indeed a very easy thing, plain and known of all men. Precisely the same thing occurs in the case of the most inspired creations of art, which are developed with such simplicity and naturalness that every one experiences the illusion of having achieved, or of being able to achieve them himself.

If ingenuous thought give the hope and the indication of the possibility of the reconciliation of unity and opposition, another form of spiritual creation, of which all have experience, provides a sort of model.   The philosopher has at his side the poet.   And the poet, too, seeks the truth; the poet, too, thirsts for the real ; he too, like the philosopher, recoils from arbitrary abstractions, because he strives towards the living and the concrete : he too, abhors the mute ecstasies of the mystics and the sentimentalists, because it is what he feels that he utters and makes to ring in the ear in beautiful words, limpid and silvery. But the poet is not condemned to the unattainable.   This very reality, torn and rent with opposition, is the object of his contemplation, and he makes it, though throbbing with opposition, yet one and undivided.   Cannot the philosopher do the same ?   Is not philosophy, like poetry, knowledge? Why should this perfection, this power of solving and of representing unity in opposition, be wanting to the philosophic concept when it is in all respects analogous to æsthetic expression? It is true that philosophy is knowledge of the universal, and therefore thought; and that poetry is knowledge of the individual, and therefore intuition and imagination. But why should not the philosophic universal, like the æsthetic expression, be both at once difference and unity, discord and concord, discrete and continuous, permanent and ever-changing? Why should reality lose its true character when mind rises from the contemplation of the particular to the contemplation of the whole? Does not the whole live in us as vividly as does the particular?

And here it is that Hegel gives his shout of jubilation, the cry of the discoverer, the *Eureka*, his principle of solution of the problem of opposites: a most simple principle, and so obvious that it deserves to be placed among those symbolized by the egg of Christopher Columbus. The opposites are not illusion, neither is unity illusion. The opposites are opposed to one another, but they are not opposed to unity. For true and concrete unity is nothing but the unity, or synthesis, of opposites. It is not immobility, it is movement. It is not fixity, but development. The philosophic concept is a concrete universal, and therefore a thinking of reality as at once united and divided. Only thus does philosophic truth correspond to poetic truth, and the pulse of thought beat with the pulse of things.

It is, indeed, the only possible solution. It rejects neither of the two preceding, which I have called "monism" and "dualism of opposites," but justifies both. It regards them as one-sided truths, fragments which await their integration in a third, in which the first and second, even the third itself, disappear, merged in the unique truth. And that truth is that unity has not opposition opposed to it, but holds it within itself; and that, without opposition, reality would not be reality, because it would not be development and life. Unity is the positive, opposition the negative; but the negative is also positive, positive in so far as negative. Were it not so, the fulness and richness of the positive would be unintelligible. If the analogy between poetry and philosophy be not satisfactory, if it be not sufficiently clear what is meant by a concrete concept, which as the logical form of development corresponds to in-

tuition as its poetical form, we might say, now
that comparisons and metaphors are more readily
chosen from the natural sciences (sacrificing
exactitude of analogy to aptness of comparison),
that the concrete universal, with its synthesis of
opposites, expresses life and not the corpse of
life; it gives the *physiology*, not the *anatomy*, of
the real.

Hegel calls his doctrine of opposites *dialectic*,
rejecting, as liable to cause misunderstandings,
the other formulae of *unity* and *coincidence of
opposites*, because in these stress is laid only upon
the unity, and not at the same time upon the
opposition. The two abstract elements, or the
opposites taken in and by themselves, he calls
moments, a figure taken from the moments of the
lever, and the word "moment" is sometimes also
applied to the third term, the synthesis. The relation of the two first to the third is expressed by
the word "solution" or "overcoming" (*Aufheben*).
And that, as Hegel intimates, means that the two
moments in their separation are both negated,
but preserved in the synthesis. The second
term (in relation to the first) appears as *negation*,
and the third (in relation to the second) as a
negation of negation, or as absolute negativity,
which is also absolute affirmation. If, for conveni-

ence of exposition, we apply numerical symbols
to this logical relation, we may call the dialectic
a *triad* or *trinity*, because it appears as composed
of three terms; but Hegel never ceases putting
us on our guard against the extrinsic and arbitrary
character of this numerical symbolism, which is
altogether unsuited to the expression of speculative truth.   And indeed, to speak accurately, in
the dialectic triad we do not think *three* concepts,
but *one* single concept, which is the concrete
universal, in its own inner nature and structure.
More than that, in order to obtain this synthesis
it is above all things necessary to define the
opposition of the terms.   And if the activity
which defines the opposition be called *intellect*,
and the activity which yields the synthesis *reason*,
it is evident that intellect is necessary to reason,
is a moment of it, is intrinsic to it; and this,
indeed, is how Hegel sometimes considers it.

Whoever cannot rise to this method of thinking opposites can make no philosophic affirmation
which is not self-contradictory and passes into
its own contrary.   This has already been ex-
emplified in the discussion of the antithesis of
monism and dualism.   And it can be seen in the
first triad of the Hegelian *Logic* : the triad which
comprehends in itself all the others, and which,

as is well known, is constituted by the terms *being*, *nothing*, and *becoming*. What is being without nothing? What is pure, indeterminate, unqualified, indistinguishable, ineffable being, *i.e.* being in general, not this or that particular being? How can it be distinguished from nothing? And, on the other hand, what is nothing without being, *i.e.* nothing conceived in itself, without determination or qualification, nothing in general, not the nothing of this or that particular thing? In what way is this distinguished from being? To take one of the terms by itself comes to the same thing as to take the other by itself, for the one has meaning only in and through the other. Thus to take the true without the false, or the good without the evil, is to make of the true something not thought (because thought is struggle against the false), and therefore something that is not true. And similarly it is to make of the good something not willed (because to will the good is to negate the evil), and therefore something that is not good. Outside the synthesis, the two terms taken abstractly pass into one another and change sides. Truth is found only in the third; that is to say, in the case of the first triad, in *becoming*, which, therefore, is, as Hegel says, "the first concrete concept."

Nevertheless, this error, which consists in taking the opposites outside the synthesis, is constantly reappearing. And against it there must always be directed the polemic which shows, as has just been shown, that outside the synthesis, the opposites are unthinkable. This polemic is the dialectic in its "subjective" or "negative" sense. But it must not be confused with the true and proper meaning of the doctrine of dialectic in its objective or positive sense, which may also be designated the logical doctrine of *development*. In this negative dialectic the result is not the synthesis, but the annulment, of the two opposite terms, each on account of the other; and therefore the terminology, which we have explained above, also acquires, like the word "dialectic" itself, a somewhat different meaning. The *intellect*, in so far as it is not an intrinsic moment of reason and inseparable from it, but is, on the contrary, the affirmation of the separate opposites which claims to stand alone as ultimate truth, intellect, in this sense, becomes a derogatory and depreciatory term. It is the *abstract intellect*, the eternal enemy of philosophic speculation. It is, at bottom, reason itself failing of its own task. "It is not the fault of the intellect if we do not proceed further, but a *subjective impotence* of reason which permits that determination to continue in that state."[1]   The triad itself gives place to a quatriad of terms: two affirmations and two negations.   Reason intervenes as negative reason, to bring confusion into the domain of intellect; but if, in this negative capacity, it prepare and compel the positive doctrine, it neither produces nor states it.

The confusion between the merely negative aspect of Hegel's dialectic and its positive content has given rise to an objection to the Hegelian doctrine of opposites, which is the battle-charger so often mounted by his adversaries: a Brigliadoro or a Bayard so very old and broken down that I do not see how any one still succeeds in keeping his seat on it.   It has been said: If being and nothing are *identical* (as Hegel proves or thinks he proves), how can they constitute becoming?   Becoming, on Hegel's theory, must be a synthesis of *opposites*, not of identities, of which there can be no synthesis. $a = a$ remains a, and does not become b.   But being is identical with nothing only when being and nothing are thought badly, or are not thought truly.   Only then does it happen that the one equals the other, not as $a = a$, but rather as

1 *Wissensch. der Logik*, iii. 48.

$o = o$. For the thought which thinks them truly, being and nothing are not identical, but precisely opposite, and in conflict with one another. And this conflict (which is also a union, since two wrestlers, in order to wrestle, must lay hold of one another!) is becoming. It is not a concept added to or derived from the first two taken in their separation, but a unique concept, outside of which there are two abstractions, two unreal shadows, being and nothing, each by itself, which are, as such, united, not by their conflict, but by their common vacuity.

Another objection, which has also seemed triumphant, consists in observing that the concrete universal, with its synthesis of opposites,—the very mark of its concreteness—is not a pure logical concept, because it tacitly introduces in the representation of movement and of development an element of sense or intuition. But if the words are given their precise significance, sense and intuition should mean something particular, individual, and historical. And what is there in the Hegelian concept of the universal which we can show to be particular, individual, or historical? What can we separate out as such an element, in the way in which, for instance, we can distinguish the particular, individual, or historical element in the empirical concept of "oak," or of "whale," or of "feudal régime"? Movement or development has about it nothing of the particular and contingent. It is a universal. It has no sense-element; it is a thought, a concept, the true concept exactly adequate to reality. Its logical theory is the concrete universal, the synthesis of opposites. But it may be that this objection was intended against the character which the concept possesses in Hegel's logic. There it is not something empty and indifferent, not a mere "recipient" ready to receive any content, but the ideal form of reality itself. And if, in this objection, "logic" is taken to be only an inconceivable abstraction, an abstraction which "is commanded," like that of mathematics, and "intuition" is taken to be the speculative concept, the criticism reveals, not a defect in Hegel, but his true glory. For it makes it clear that he has destroyed that false concept of a barren and formal logic as an arbitrary abstraction, and to the true logical concept he has given a character of concreteness, which can also be called "intuition," when intuition signifies, as we showed above, that philosophy must spring from the bosom of divine Poetry, *matre pulchra filia pulchrior.*

Philosophy, thus set in friendly relations with poetry, enters that state which in these days of Nietzschian phraseology is called "dionysiac." It is a state to terrify timid thinkers, who, however, in so far as they philosophize, find themselves, without knowing it, in the same condition. Thus our Rosmini, aghast at the dialectic of being and not being, exclaimed : "And even were it as true, as it is false, that being can deny itself, the question would always recur : what could move it to deny itself? What reason could be assigned for this alleged desire, on the part of being, to deny itself and to ignore itself? why, in short, should it make this mad effort to annul itself? for the system of Hegel does nothing less than *make being go mad and introduce madness into all things.* Thus he claims to give them life, movement, free passage, becoming. I do not know if a similar effort was ever made in the world, to make all things, even being itself, go mad." [1]   Probably Rosmini did not remember that the same description, though certainly in far better style, had been given by Hegel himself in the *Phenomenology*, when, having represented the movement of reality,—that process of coming

[1] *Saggio storico-critico sulle categorie e la dialettica,* posthumous work (Turin, 1883), p. 371.

into being and passing away which itself is without beginning and without end—he concluded
with the words : " The true is the Bacchic delirium, in which not one of its components is not
drunk ; and since each becomes immediately dissolved when the others withdraw,—that delirium
is also simple and transparent repose." [1]   Reality
seems mad, because it is life : philosophy seems
mad, because it breaks up abstractions and lives
that life in thought.   It is a madness which is
the highest wisdom, and the true and not meta-
phorical madmen are they who become mad with
the empty words of semi-philosophy, who take
formulas for reality, who never succeed in raising
themselves to that clear sky whence they can see
their work as it really is.   They see the sky above
their heads, unattainable by them, and are ready
to call it a madhouse.

Another manifestation of this same irrational
fear is the cry that, with such logic as this, the
very base and rule of man's thought is taken from
him—the principle of identity and contradiction.
Proofs are cited in Hegel's frequent outbursts of
ill-humour against this principle and in his saying that for it there should be substituted the
opposite principle : that everything is self-contra-

---

[1] *Phänom. d. Geistes,*[2] p. 37.

dictory. But things do not stand precisely in this case. Hegel does not deny the principle of identity, for otherwise he would have been obliged to admit that his logical theory was at once true and not true, true and false; that philosophically, being and nothing could be thought in the synthesis, and also, each in and for itself, outside the synthesis. And all his polemic, all his philosophy, would no longer have any meaning; it would never have been seriously accomplished; whereas, obviously, it is most serious. So far from destroying the principle of identity, Hegel gives it new life and force, makes it what truly it ought to be and what in ordinary thought it is not. For in ordinary thought, in semi-philosophy, reality is left divided, as has been seen, into two parts. Now it is the one, now the other, and when it is the one, it is not the other. And yet, in this effort after exclusion, the one passes into the other and both are fused in nothingness. It is these truly unthinkable contradictions that ordinary thought claims to justify and embellish by adducing the principle of identity. If attention be paid to the words of Hegel alone, we might say that he does not believe in the principle of identity; but if we look closer, we see that what Hegel does not believe in is the *fallacious use of*

the principle of identity—the use made of it by those
abstract thinkers who retain unity by cancelling
opposition, or retain opposition by cancelling
unity; or, as he says, the principle of identity
taken as a "law of the abstract intellect." That
fallacious use exists, because we are unwilling to
recognize that opposition or contradiction is not a
defect, or a stain, or an evil in things, which could
be eliminated from them, far less a subjective
error of ours; but that it is indeed the true being
of things. All things are contradictory in themselves, and thought must think this contradiction.
This establishes truly and firmly the principle of
identity, which triumphs over opposition in thinking it, that is to say, in grasping it in its unity.
Opposition thought is opposition *overcome*, and
overcome precisely in virtue of the principle of
identity. Opposition unrecognized, or unity unrecognized, is apparent obedience to the principle,
but in effect is its real contradiction. There is
the same difference between Hegel's method of
thinking and the method of ordinary thought as
there is between him who confronts and conquers
an enemy and him who closes his eyes in order
not to see him, and believing that he has thus got
rid of him, becomes his victim. "Speculative
thought consists in determining opposition as

thought does, and in so doing it determines itself. It does not, like representative thought, allow itself to be dominated by opposition into resolving its own determinations only in other determinations or in nothingness."[1] Reality is a nexus of opposites, and is not rendered dissipated and discrete thereby. Indeed, it is in and through opposition that reality eternally generates itself. Nor does thought, which is supreme reality, the reality of reality, become dissipated or discrete, but it grasps unity in opposition and logically synthesizes it.

The dialectic of Hegel, like all discoveries of truth, does not come to drive preceding truths from their place, but to confirm and to enrich them. The concrete universal, unity in distinction and in opposition, is the true and complete principle of identity, which allows no separate existence, either as complement or rival to the principle enunciated in older doctrines, because it has absorbed the older principle into itself and has transformed it into its own flesh and blood.

[1] *Wissensch. d. Logik*, ii. 67-8.

II

EXPLANATIONS RELATING TO THE HISTORY OF THE DIALECTIC

SOME historians of philosophy have thought that the problem of opposites was the whole problem of philosophy. Hence the history of the various attempts at a solution of this problem has sometimes been taken for the whole history of philosophy, and the one has been narrated in place of the other. But the dialectic, so far from being the whole of philosophy, is not even the whole of logic; although it is a most important part of it, and might be called its crown.

The reason for this confusion will perhaps be evident from what was said above. It lies in the intimate connexion between the logical problem of opposites and the great disputes of the monists and the dualists, of the materialists and the spiritualists. These disputes form the

principal part of the treatises and histories of
philosophy, although they do not constitute its
primary and fundamental task, which is better
expressed by the phrase "know thyself." But
this apparent coincidence will disappear, when
we consider that to think logically and to
construct a logical theory of logic, are two
different things; that it is one thing to think
dialectically, and another to have logical consciousness of dialectical thought. Were this
not so, the Hegelian solution would have already
been finally given by the many philosophers
who have in fact thought reality dialectically,
or at least given on the occasions when they
have thought it in that way. Doubtless, every
philosophic problem calls up all the others. All
can be discovered implicit in each one, and in
the solution, true or false, of one problem, there
is the solution, true or false, of all. But if it is
impossible altogether to separate the histories
of individual philosophic problems from one
another, it is also true that these problems are
distinct; and we should not confuse the various
members of the organic whole, if we do not
wish to lose all idea of that whole itself.

This principle we must bear in mind, if we
are to circumscribe the enquiry as to the

historical development of the dialectic doctrine of opposites, and thereby to recognize the place and originality that belong to the thought of Hegel. This enquiry, within these precise limits, has perhaps not yet been carried out in a suitable way. This is due also to the fact that the general consciousness of those who cultivate philosophic studies has not been persuaded of the importance and truth of the doctrine, so that there have been wanting the necessary interest and the directive criterion for research into its history. The best that has been collected on this theme, is to be found in the books of Hegel himself, especially in his *History of Philosophy* ;[1] and here it is opportune rapidly to review his scattered remarks, making, where necessary, some additions and some comments.

Was Hegel the first to formulate the logical principle of the dialectic and of its development? Had he forerunners, and if so, who were they? Through what forms and through what approxi-

---

[1] See also the historical introduction to the *Logik u. Metaphysik* of Kuno Fischer (2nd ed., 1865), and the *Prolusione ed introduzione alle lezioni di filosofia* of B. Spaventa (Napoli, 1862 ; reprinted by Gentile with the new title : *La Filosofia italiana nelle sue relazioni con la filosofia europea*, Bari, 1908). For the immediate antecedents of the Hegelian dialectic and for the various phases of its development, see preferably Al. Schmid, *Entwickelungsgeschicte der hegelschen Logik* (Regensburg, 1858).

mations did that principle pass, prior to attaining in him to its perfection?

The doctrine of dialectic is the work of mature thought, the product of long philosophic incubation. In Hellenic antiquity we find, in Zeno of Elea's refutations of the reality of motion, the first perception of the difficulties to which the principle of opposites gives rise. Motion is the very fact of development in the form in which it offers itself most easily to reflexion. And Zeno, having set the difficulties in very clear relief, resolved the contradiction by denying the reality of movement. (His arguments of the arrow, of Achilles and the tortoise, etc., showed the contradictions involved in space and time.) Motion is an illusion of the senses; being, reality, is one and immovable. In opposition to Zeno, Heraclitus made of movement and becoming the true reality. His sayings are: "being and not-being are the same," "all is, and also is not," "everything flows." His comparisons of things with a river, of the opposite which is in its opposite as sweet and bitter are in honey, of the bow and of the lyre; his cosmological views of war and peace, of discord and harmony, show how profoundly Heraclitus felt reality as contradiction and

development. Hegel used to say that there
was not one affirmation of Heraclitus that he
had not incorporated in his own logic. But it
is to be observed, that by the very act of
incorporating them in his doctrine, he conferred
upon these affirmations a far more precise
signification than they had possessed when they
stood alone. Without doubt we must hold them
in high esteem, just as they have been handed
down, an ingenuous and penetrating vision of
the truth. But we must not insist upon them
too much, lest we should run the risk of
historical falsification, and make a Post-Kantian
of a Pre-Socratic.

The same remark applies to the Platonic
dialectic of the *Parmenides*, the *Sophist*, the
Philebus, dialogues whose interpretation and
historical place are matters of much dispute.
Hegel thought that they contained the essence
of the Platonic philosophy, the attempt, *i.e.* to
pass from the universal, still as yet abstract, to
the concrete universal, to posit the speculative
form of the concept as unity in diversity.
Questions are discussed there concerning the
one and the many, identity and non-identity,
motion and rest, coming into being and passing
away, being and not being, finite and infinite,

the limited and the unlimited. The conclusion of the *Parmenides* is, that the one is and is not, is itself and other than itself, and that things in relation to themselves and in distinction from others are and are not, appear and do not appear. And all of this indicates an attempt to overcome a difficulty, which issues only in a negative result. In any case, as Hegel noted, in Plato we find the dialectic, but not yet complete consciousness of its nature. It is a speculative method of thinking, greatly superior in value to the argumentations of the Sophists or to the later ingenuities of the Sceptics : but it does not attain to the level of logical doctrine. Of Aristotle, it may be said that his logical consciousness is in disagreement with his speculative consciousness : his logic is purely intellectualist, his metaphysic is a study of the categories.

We can discover nothing more than an extremity of need, or perhaps a conscious-ness of helplessness and an indication of the lacuna, in the doctrines of Philo the Jew and of the Gnostics. For them, true reality, absolute being, is considered unattainable by thought—the ineffable, inscrutable God, the abyss where all is negated. This is equally true of Plotinus, for whom all predicates are inadequate to the Absolute, each of them expressing but a determination of it.   In Proclus is developed an idea that Plato had already mentioned—the idea of the trinity or the triad.   This idea, and the idea of the Absolute as spirit, is the great philosophic advance implicit in Christianity.

Nicholas of Cusa, inheriting Neoplatonic and mystical traditions, was the thinker who, at the beginning of the modern world, most energetically expressed the need of the human spirit to emerge from dualisms and conflicts, and to raise itself to that simplicity where opposites coincide.   And the Cusan was the first to perceive that this coincidence of opposites is in antithesis to the merely abstract logic of Aristotle, who conceived contrariety as perfect difference,[1] and did not admit that unity could contain contraries, since he regarded each thing as the privation of its opposite.   Cusanus maintained against this, that unity is prior to duality, the coincidence of opposites prior to their separation.   But in his view, that which unites the opposites, thought as simple coincidence, is incomprehensible to man, either by sense, or by reason, or by intellect, which are the three forms of the human mind.   It remains a simple limit; and of God,

---

[1] Ἡ ἐναντιότης ἐστὶ διαφορὰ τέλειος, *Metaphys.* 1055 a.

who is a union of all contraries, no other knowledge is permitted, save an incomprehensible
comprehension, a learned ignorance.[1]

His thought seems to assume a more positive
function in Giordano Bruno, who proclaims
himself a disciple of " the divine Cusan." Bruno
also upholds the coincidence of opposites as the
best principle of a philosophy that has been
forgotten and must be resuscitated; and gives
an eloquent description of the unification of
contraries, of. the perfect circle and of the
straight line, of the acute and obtuse angle, of
heat and cold, of corruption and generation, of
love and hate, of poison and antidote, of the
spherical and the plane, of the concave and the
convex, of wrath and patience, of pride and
humility, of avarice and liberality. And there
is an echo of the Cusan in these memorable
words : " Whoever wishes to know the greatest
secrets of nature, let him study and contemplate
the least and the greatest of contraries and
opposites. Profound is the magic that knows how
to draw the contrast, after having found the point
of union. This was the direction of Aristotle's
thought, when he posited privation, conjoined

---

[1] On the Cusan, see Fiorentino, *Il Risorgimento filosofico nel
Quattrocento* (Napoli, 1885), cap. ii.

with a determinate disposition, as the progenitrix, parent and mother of form; but he could never attain to it. He could not, because stopping at the *genus* of opposition, he was hampered in such a way that he failed to descend to the *species* of contrariety, so that he did not attain, did not even fix his eyes upon the goal. Hence he erred at every step, through saying that the contraries could not truly come together in the same subject." In his naturalistic intuition, the principle of the coincidence of opposites becomes to Bruno a kind of æsthetic principle of contemplation: "We delight in colour, not in one specific colour, whatever it may be, but chiefly in one, which weaves into itself all colours. We delight in a voice, not in a single voice, but in one complex sound which results from the harmony of many voices. We delight in a sensible, but chiefly in that which comprehends in itself all sensibles; in a knowable which comprehends in itself every knowable; in an apprehensible, which embraces all that can be understood; in a being which completes the whole, but chiefly in that which is the whole itself." [1]   The principle is no longer beyond

---

[1] *De la causa principio ed uno*, Dialogue V., in fine (*V. Dialoghi metafisici*, ed. Gentile, Bari, Laterza), 1907, pp. 255-257.

man's reach; it is a power of the human mind; though not yet a rigorously logical power. It still awaits its justification in a doctrine of the concept.

The unity of opposites is also earnestly asserted by the *philosophus theutonicus*, Jacob Böhme. He posits the antitheses in their full force, says Hegel, but does not allow his thought to be arrested by the strength of the differences, and proceeds to posit unity. For him, the "yes" is unknowable without the "no." The One, God, is in himself unknowable. If he is to be known, he must distinguish himself from himself, the Father must duplicate himself in the Son. Böhme sees the triad in all things, and fathoms the significance of the Christian trinity, but he too does not succeed in putting his thoughts into the form proper to thought.

The philosophy of the seventeenth and eighteenth centuries which developed under the influence of the mathematical science of nature, was not capable even of setting the problem in the form proper to thought. For Descartes, thought and extension unite in God, but in an incomprehensible manner. For Spinoza, they unite in Substance: but "mode," which is the third term after substance and attribute, does not constitute a dialectic synthesis.   Leibniz is wrecked on the problem of evil and arrives at an optimism of but slight philosophical value. The popular philosophy of the eighteenth century resolves all antitheses in God, who thus becomes an assemblage of contradictions, the problem of problems.   Only here and there do we find in some solitary thinker hints and suggestions of the dialectic solution.   For example, there is the *philosophus italicus*, G. B. Vico, who not only actually thinks history and life dialectically, but recoils from the logic of Aristotle, and from that of Cartesian physics and mathematics, founding on the one hand a logic of fancy (poetic logic), and of history (logic of certainty); on the other he gives importance to the inductive logic of observation and of experiment, as presage of a more concrete logic. Another solitary figure, in many respects akin to Vico, John George Hamann (who was said by Jacobi to unite in himself in a high degree all extremes) showed himself from youth onwards dissatisfied with the principles of identity and reason and attracted by that of the *coincidentia oppositorum*.   Hamann had met with this principle in the *De triplici minimo et mensura* of Bruno; and he had carried it "for years in his head

without being able either to forget it or to understand it." Yet it seemed to him to be "the
sole sufficient reason of all contradictions and
the true process of their solution and levelling,"
which would put an end to all the contests of the
abstract thinkers.[1] From Hamann knowledge
of this principle passed to Jacobi, who published
the extracts relating to it which are to be found
in the works of Bruno. But Jacobi, hampered
by his theory of immediate knowledge, though
he indicated the lacuna, was not himself in
a position to pass beyond it by strict logical
thought.

The reason for this is, that in order to arrive
at a truly logical statement of the problem of
opposites, and to escape the mystical and agnostic
solution (which indeed was no solution), it was
necessary that the Kantian revolution should
be accomplished. It was Kant, — although
his whole *Critique of Pure Reason* seemed to
Hamann much less important than the sole
pronouncement of Bruno on the *principium
coincidentiae oppositorum* — who was precisely in
virtue of that *critique*, the true progenitor of the
new principle of the coincidence of opposites,

---

[1] For Hamann, cf. Hegel, *Vermischte Schriften*, ii. 36-37, 87-88,
and the Essays collected in B. Croce, *Saggi fil.* iii.

of the new dialectic, that is, of the logical doctrine of dialectic.

It is true that Kant, like his immediate precursors, from Descartes to Leibniz and to Hume, was under the influence of the prevailing intellectualism and of the ideal of a mathematical science of nature. Hence his agnosticism, the phantom of the thing-in-itself, the abstractness of the categorical imperative, and his respect for traditional logic. But at the same time, he maintains and renders more effective the difference between intellect and reason. In the *Critique of Judgment* he propounds a mode of thinking reality, which is no longer merely mechanical, no longer either the external teleology of the eighteenth century, but is genuine *internal* teleology; he catches sight of the idea beyond the abstract concept. Better still, in his exposition of the Antinomies, Kant advances the problem of opposites a stage further. The Antinomies certainly seem insoluble, but the contradictions spring directly from the necessities of the human mind. What is more important (what indeed is his true glory), he discovers the *a priori synthesis*; and that, as Hegel observed, can be nothing but " an original synthesis of opposites." With Kant this synthesis does not

receive its full value.   It is not developed in the
dialectic triad.   But once it had been brought to
light, it could not be slow to reveal the riches
which it contained in itself.   The *a priori synthesis*
is the source of transcendental logic, which exists
by the side of the old logic, at first parallel to
it, but inevitably bound to end by destroying it.
Kant also throws into relief the form of triplicity,
and although he employs it in an altogether extrinsic manner, yet he does employ it constantly,
and almost with the presentiment of its near and
greater destinies.

The task that awaited philosophy after Kant
seems evident : to develop the *a priori synthesis*,
to create the new philosophical logic, to solve the
problem of opposites, by destroying the dualisms
that had not only been left intact, but rendered
more powerful, by Kant.   And if there be little
more in Fichte than there was in Kant, yet in
him everything becomes more simple and more
transparent.   The thing-in-itself is denied.   But
on the other hand the concept of the Ego retains
a subjective significance, and does not accomplish
the true unity of subject and object, so that Fichte
does not succeed in justifying nature in relation
to spirit, and ends, like Kant, in moral abstractness and in faith.   But the idea of a new

Logic is better determined, so much so that philosophy is conceived as a *doctrine of science*; and the form of triplicity assumes a dominant position, as thesis, antithesis and synthesis. Schelling takes another step forward, in arriving at the conviction that it is not possible to think philosophically, except through the principle of identity of opposites; for he conceives the Absolute as identity of opposites. But for him the Absolute is indifference of subject and object. Its differences are merely quantitative. It is not yet subject and spirit. And his theory of knowledge is without logic, because for him the instrument of philosophy is æsthetic contemplation. This deficiency Schelling never succeeded in overcoming, and the consequences were so serious as to give rise to what has been called his second manner, the metaphysic of the irrational.

Hegel, as is known, appeared later in the philosophical world than his young contemporary Schelling, whose disciple in a certain sense he may be called. But what for Schelling was the point of arrival, was for Hegel a point of transition; what was for Schelling the final phase, whence began the process of his degeneration, was for Hegel a juvenile phase. He too for some time

knew no other instrument of philosophy than æsthetic contemplation, knew intuition as intellectual
intuition, and knew no other philosophical system
than the work of art. He too (in the first sketch of
his system that has been preserved) placed at the
summit of spiritual development, not philosophy,
but religion. But the profound scientific spirit
of Hegel led him gradually to recognize that
philosophy cannot have any other form than that
of thought, in the precise sense in which thought
differs from fancy and intuition. Certainly, it
was no longer thought in the old logico-natural-
istic sense: after Kant, Fichte and Schelling,
that was no longer a possible meaning: the
intellectualism of the two preceding centuries
had been mortally wounded. There must be a
logical form, which should preserve and reinforce
the recent conquests of philosophy; a logical
form, which should be the form of the real in its
integrity. Everything urged Hegel into this
path of enquiry; his admiration for the harmony
of the Hellenic world; his participation in the
romantic movement, so rich in antitheses; his
theological studies, from which it seemed to him
that the Christian idea of the Trinity, attenuated
or rendered void by Protestant rationalism, should
find its refuge and its true meaning in the

new philosophy; his speculative studies on the
Kantian synthesis and antinomies. And with
the *Phenomenology of Spirit* (1807), he detached
himself from the philosophical tendencies to
which he had previously adhered, and brought
to light his principle of solution of the problem
of opposites :— no longer a simple coincidence
in a third unknown or unintelligible term; no
longer motionless unity; no longer the intuition
of Schelling; but unity and diversity together,
movement and dialectic. The preface to the
Phenomenology has been called " Hegel's farewell
to Romanticism"; but the truth is that it was
only because of his secession that Romanticism
was saved for philosophy. Only a romantic who
had in a certain sense surpassed Romanticism
could pluck its philosophical fruit.

The logic of the dialectic is therefore to be
considered a true and original discovery of
Hegel, not only in comparison with his remote
predecessors, but also with those who are nearest
to him. If a proof of this be sought, one need
only consider his attitude towards these latter.
Kant, who disclaimed Fichte, would have disclaimed Hegel even more decisively. In Kant's
philosophy there were not the necessary conditions for understanding Hegel, and therefore

there could be no true criticism. But Hegel, who combated in a definitive manner the erroneous tendencies and aspects of the Kantian philosophy, and all the obsolete views which appeared in its train, was also the man who showed what a new and fruitful contribution it had made to philosophy. So true is this that it has been possible to say that no one but Hegel has understood Kant.[1] Schelling always remained deaf and hostile to the conception of his former friend ; and during the half century that he survived, he obstinately opposed to it his own theory, grown old and degenerate. Sometimes, indeed (as in the celebrated preface to the *Fragments* of Cousin), while violently rejecting the philosophy of Hegel, in the same breath he complained that he had been robbed by him : without however anywhere clearly formulating either the nature of the theft, or the error. Hegel, on the other hand, always venerated Schelling as " the father of the new philosophy." He recognized the gleam of dialectic that there was in him, and always calmly pointed out his merits and his

---

[1] " For my part, I have to declare that, so far as it has been given me to see, I have no evidence that any man has thoroughly understood Kant except Hegel, or that this latter himself remains aught else than a problem whose solution has been arrogated, but never effectuated " (J. H. Stirling, *The Secret of Hegel*, London, 1865, i. 1.;).

defects.   If a superior point of view show itself such by comprehending within it those that are inferior; if the proof of the truth of a doctrine lie in its power of furnishing at once the justification of truths discovered by others and the explication of their errors; then this sort of proof has not been wanting to the doctrine of Hegel. Kant did not fully understand himself, and fell into the arms of the neocriticists, who turned from his transcendental logic to merely naturalistic logic; Schelling did not fully understand himself and ended with little credit as the second Schelling.   But for Hegel, both ended in his great mind, who was their spiritual son : an end more worthy than that of serving as an exercise for little scholars, or of surviving each by himself in the failure to know himself.

III

THE DIALECTIC AND
THE CONCEPTION OF REALITY

To think dialectically, and to think the logical theory of the dialectic, are, then, two distinct mental acts. Yet it is clear that the second act strengthens the first, by giving it consciousness of itself and freeing it from the embarrassments that arise from false ideas concerning the nature of philosophic truth. This is precisely what occurs in the case of Hegel. He is not only the great theorist of the dialectic form of thought, but the most complete dialectician who has appeared in history. His dialectical treatment of the ordinary conception of reality modifies it in several parts and changes its general aspect. All the dualities, all the fissures, all the *hiatus*, and, so to speak, all the rents and wounds with which reality shows itself to be lacerated by the abstract intellect, are filled, closed and healed. A complete unity

(*gediegene Einheit*) is realized : the coherence of
the organic whole is re-established ; blood and
life again circulate within it.

And we must note above all that there disappears a series of dualisms, which are not true
opposites, not even true distincts. They are
false opposites and false distincts, terms which
cannot be thought either as elements constitutive
of the concept as universal, or as its particular
forms, for the simple reason that, as formulated,
they do not exist. Hegel (who, in his criticism,
refers here and there to the difference between
them and genuine distincts and opposites) exactly
determines their genesis, which is to be found in
the phantasmagorias of abstraction. They are
dualities of terms, which have their origin in the
empirical sciences, in the perceptive and legislative
consciousness, in the sciences of phenomena.
These sciences, just because they are immersed in
phenomena, whenever they attempt to rise to the
universal are compelled to break up reality into
appearance and *essence*, *external* and *internal*,
accident and *substance*, *manifestation* and *force*,
finite and *infinite*, *many* and *one*, *sensible* and *super-
sensible*, *matter* and *spirit*, and such like terms.
Were these terms truly distinct (or if they truly
designated distincts), they would give rise to the

problem of the conjunction of distincts in the concrete concept. Were they true opposites, really opposed (or if they designated things truly and really opposed),[1] they would give rise to the problem of the synthesis of opposites. But, since they are not, since they assume their appearance of distinction and opposition, only through the arbitrary abstraction of the empiricists, naturalists and mathematicians, criticism of them, achieved by a negative dialectic, is accomplished by a different process from that which directs positive dialectic.

They are, in truth, unthinkable; and every attempt to overcome the duality, by insisting upon either of the two terms, as it appears in distinction from the other, ends by changing it into the other. Materialism preserves the phenomenon, matter, the finite, the sensible, the external, etc. ; but, since that term is naturally so constituted as to require its other, the infinite appears again in that finite, assuming the form of a quantitative infinite, of a finite from which another finite is born, then another finite, then another, to infinity. This is what Hegel called the false or *bad infinite*. Supernaturalism pre-

---

[1] These and similar reservations are made necessary by the plurality of meanings which those words have had in philosophical language.

serves the other term as sole reality ; but essence
without appearance, the internal without the
external, the infinite without the finite, become
something inscrutable and unknowable. Here
appears the *thing-in-itself*, which would better be
called *vacuity in itself* : the great mystery, which
(Hegel says) is a very easy thing to know ;
because not only is the thing-in-itself not outside
thought, but on the contrary is a product of
thought, of thought which has been pushed on to
pure abstraction, and which takes as its object
empty identity with itself. The thing-in-itself,
from its very inanity, leads back to the phenomenon, to the finite, to the external, as alone
real and thinkable ; and precisely in as much as
it is phenomenon, it is finite and external.

The positive correction is given by the
concrete concept, by that character of concreteness, proper to the Hegelian concept and
differentiating it from naturalistic and mathematical abstractions. The real is neither of those
terms ; nor is it their sum : it is the concrete
concept, which fills the emptiness of the thing in
itself and annihilates the distance, which had
separated that from the phenomenon. It is the
absolute, which is no longer a parallelism of
attributes or an indifference to both ; but which

accentuates and confers new significance on one
of the terms, which, in virtue of that new
significance, absorbs and brings the other within
itself. Thus substance becomes subject, the
absolute determines itself as spirit and idea; and
materialism is overcome. Thus too reality is
no longer an internal confronting an external:
nature (according to the saying of Goethe, which
Hegel accepts and makes his own) has neither
nut nor shell, but is all of a piece. The one is
not beyond the many, but is the many; spirit is
not beyond body, but is body. And supernaturalism is overcome.[1]

With the destruction of these false distinctions
and oppositions, which may all be summarily
represented by the duality of essence and
appearance, there is connected the purely dialectic
treatment (the positive dialectic) of true oppositions. These may be summarily represented by the
antithetic duality of being and not-being. This is
a dualism founded upon real opposition; for no
one could think of denying the existence of evil,
of the false, of the ugly, of the irrational, of death,
and the antithesis of these terms to the good, to the
true, to the beautiful, to the rational and to life.

---

[1] For the criticism of these concepts, see especially the doctrine of
the Essence, which forms the second part of the *Logic*.

Nor does Hegel deny it. But owing to his
logical doctrine, which sees in the very act of
thinking opposites, the conception of reality itself
as development, he cannot consider the negative
term, the side of not-being, as something opposed
to and separated from the other. If the negative
term did not exist, development would not exist ;
reality, and with it, the positive term, would disappear. The negative is the spring of development ; opposition is the very soul of the real.
The lack of all contact with error is not thought
and is not truth ; but is the absence of thought,
and therefore of truth. Innocence is a characteristic, not of action, but of inaction : he who acts,
errs ; but he who acts is at grips with evil. A
true felicity, a felicity that is truly human or
manly, is not a beatitude that knows no suffering.
Such a beatitude would be possible only to
fatuity and imbecility ; and the conditions of it
find no place in the history of a world which,
where strife is wanting (says Hegel), " shows its
pages blank."

If this be true (as it doubtless is, in accordance with the general and profound persuasion of
humanity, expressed in many aphorisms, which
seem sometimes to be Hegelian phrases), the
relation between the ideal and the real, the

rational and the real, cannot be understood in the sense that these words bear in the philosophy of the schools; that is, as the conflict between a rational which is not real and a real which is not rational. *What is real is rational, and what is rational is real.*[1] The idea and the fact are the same. What, for instance, do we call rational in the domain of scientific thought, but thought itself? An irrational thought is not thought; as thought it is unreal. What do we call rational in the domain of artistic production? The work of art itself: an artistic fact, if it were ugly, would not be artistic fact; it is certainly no artistic "reality," which includes the "note" of ugliness; but artistic unreality. What is called irrational, is, then, the unreal; and cannot be considered as a species or class of real objects. Without doubt, even unreality has its reality, but it is the reality of unreality, the reality which belongs to not-being in the dialectic triad, to the nothing which is not the real, but the stimulus of the real, the spring of development.

Those who, relying on this doctrine of the identity of the real and the rational, have applied the term optimism to the Hegelian conception of reality and of life, have grossly misunderstood his

---

[1] Preface to the *Philosophy of Rights*; and cf. *Encycl.* § 6.

meaning. Hegel cancels neither the evil nor the
ugly, nor the false nor the vain : *nothing could be
more alien to his conception of reality, so dramatic,
and in a certain sense so tragic.* What he sets
himself to do is to understand the function of evil
and of error ; and to understand it as evil and as
error is surely not to deny it as such, but rather
to strengthen it. To do this is not to close one's
eyes upon the sad spectacle, or to falsify it with
the puerile justifications of the external teleology
of the eighteenth century (as, for instance, did
Bernardin de Saint-Pierre). But the truth at
the bottom of this superficial ascription of
optimism to Hegel is that he cannot be called a
pessimist ; because pessimism is the negation of
the positive term in the dyad of opposites, just as
optimism is the negation of the negative term.
And indeed, have there ever been or can there
ever be self-consistent optimists or pessimists ?
No more than there have been self-consistent
monists or dualists. Every optimist has a pessimistic side ; just as every pessimist proposes a
method of liberation from evil and from error,
and therefore has his optimistic side. Good and
evil are opposed and correlative terms ; and the
affirmation of the one is the affirmation of the
other. Hegel, who denies both, while preserving

both in the dialectic synthesis, is beyond both
optimism and pessimism, high up on that
philosophic Olympus, where there is neither
laughter nor tears; for laughter and tears have
become objects for spirit, and their agitation is
overcome in the serenity of thought, as in the
concreteness of life.

Fact, reality, is always rational and ideal;
it is always truth, always wisdom and moral
goodness. But, be it well understood, by fact
is meant what is really fact; by reality, what
is truly reality. The illogical, the unpleasing,
the ugly, the base, the capricious, is not fact,
but the absence of fact, it is void, not-being; at
most it is the demand for true being, the stimulus
to reality, not reality itself. Hegel never
dreamed of accepting and justifying as fact what
is misplaced and perverted; and may this not
be his justification for considering it, as he
considers it, unreality and void? As the old
saying has it, Nature abhors a void; but man
most certainly does so, because the void is the
death of his activity, *i.e.* of his being as man.

If Hegel's philosophy furnishes the justification, not of evil, but only of the function of
evil, on the other hand he was never weary of
warning against the facility and superficiality

with which people are wont to declare irrational
that . which effectually has been and is, and
which, in virtue of this effective existence,
cannot be considered irrational. Hegel is the
great enemy of the discontented with life, of
those sensitive souls who perpetually declaim
and agitate in the name of reason and virtue,
and (to take an historical example) of *Faustism*,
which proclaims that theory is grey and the tree
of life green, which rebels against the laws of
custom and of existence, which despises truth
and science, and instead of being possessed by
the celestial spirit, falls into the power of the
earthly spirit. He is the enemy of *encyclopaedic
humanitarianism* and of *Jacobinism*, which
opposes its own exquisite heart to hard reality,
and sees everywhere the tyranny and roguery
of priests and despots ; and of *Kantian abstractness*, of a duty which is always outside human
feeling. He hates that virtue, which is always
at strife with the course of the world ; which
brings stones to birth that it may dash itself
against them ; which never knows just what
it wishes ; which certainly has a big head, but
big because it is swelled, and which, if it be
seriously occupied with anything, is occupied
with admiring its own unapproachable and

moving perfection. He hates the *Sollen*, the ought to be, the impotence of the ideal, which always ought to be and never is, which never finds a reality adequate to it, when, as a matter of fact, all reality is adequate to the ideal. The destiny of that "ought to be" is to become wearisome, as do all the most beautiful words (Justice, Virtue, Duty, Morality, Liberty, etc.), in the mouths of those for whom they are mere words, resounding in noisy barrenness, where others act who do not fear to soil the purity of the idea by translating it into deed. In the strife between the "ought to be," between this vain virtue and the course of the world, the course of the world always wins. For either the course of the world does not change and the demands of virtue reveal themselves as arbitrary and absurd, and therefore as not truly virtuous : at the most they are good intentions, perhaps excellent intentions ; but "the laurels of good intentions are dry leaves, which have never been green." Or else, the end of virtue is achieved, it enters into and becomes part of the world's course ; and what dies in this case is not the course of the world, but virtue, separated from the actual ; unless indeed it is willing to continue living, in order to sulk at its

ideal for having been guilty of becoming real!
The illusion arises from the struggle, which is
certainly real; but not as the struggle of the
individual with the world, but as the struggle
of the world with itself, of the world that makes
itself. "Each one wills and believes himself
better than the world in which he is; but he
who is better, only expresses his world better
than others express it."[1]

What then is this repugnance of the bearers
of ideal towards the actual, of the admirers of
the universal towards individuality? Individuality is nothing but the vehicle of universality,
the process of its becoming effective. Nothing
can be achieved if it does not become a passion
of man: *nothing great can be done without
passion*. And passion is activity, which is
directed toward particular interests and ends.
So much is it true that particular interest is
the vehicle of the universal, that men by the
very pursuit of their own private ends realize
the universal. For instance, one man makes
a slave of another, and from the strife between
slave and master, there arises in both the true

---

[1] From the aphorisms, to be found in the appendix of Rosenkranz's
Hegel's Leben, p. 550.—For the satire on the *Sollen* see especially the
Phenomenology, section *Vernunft*, B, and the introduction to the
Philosophy of History.

idea of liberty and of humanity. Their actions achieve more than their conscious intentions, and fulfil the immanent intentions, the intentions of reason, which avails itself of them; this is the cunning of reason (*die List der Vernunft*). This must not be understood in a transcendental sense. The cunning of reason is the imaginative phrase which denotes the rationality of all that man truly does (of any human work whatsoever), whether or no he has reflective consciousness of it. Thus the artist creates the work of art and does not understand the completed work; yet, though he fail to understand it, his work is not irrational, for it obeys the supreme rationality of genius. Thus the good and ingenuously heroic soul believes that it simply obeys the impulse of its own individual sentiment; it is not conscious of its action in the way in which the observer and the historian are conscious of it later; and it is not for this reason less good and less heroic. Great men take the very will of reason, what is real and substantial in the wants of their time and people, and make of them their own individual passion, their own peculiar interest: they are the "men of affairs" of the world-spirit. And this is precisely the reason why

those who judge them superficially never succeed
in discovering in them anything but mean
motives. They see no other aspect of their
work than the personal, although that is
essential; and thus they justify the proverb
that no man is a hero to his valet; and this
is true, as Hegel observes (and Goethe takes
pleasure in repeating the acute remark), not
because the great man is not a great man, but
because the valet is a valet. For this reason,
honours and gratitude are not usually accorded
to great men by their contemporaries; nor do
they receive this satisfaction at the hands of
the public opinion of posterity. What falls to
them is not honour, but *immortal glory*; they
live in the spirit of those very people who strove
with them, and who yet are full of them.

This Hegelian manner of considering life,
translated into terms of current politics, has been
held to be a conservative spirit. For this reason
it has been said that just as Rousseau was the
philosopher of the French Revolution, so Hegel
was the special philosopher of the Prussian
Restoration, the philosopher of the secret council
of government and of the bureaucratic ruling of
the state. But without going into the question
of the greater or less truth in fact of these affirma-

tions, it is important to distinguish between the historical Hegel and the philosopher Hegel. The historical individual, the Hegel who took part, under certain determinate conditions, in the social and political problems of his time and of his nation,—the Hegel who belongs to the biographer and the political historian,—must not be confused with the philosopher Hegel, who alone belongs to the historian of philosophy. The position from which a particular political attitude can be deduced shows by that very fact that it is not pure philosophical truth. Philosophy should not meddle (observed the same Hegel) with things that do not concern it ; and therefore Plato might well have spared himself the trouble of giving advice to nurses on the way they should carry children in their arms ; and Fichte, of " constructing " a model police passport, which should be furnished, according to him, not only with particulars as to its bearer, but also with his portrait. Hegel's conception of life was so philosophical that conservatism, revolution, and restoration, each in turn, finds its justification in it. On this point the socialist Engels and the conservative historian Treitschke [1] are in agreement ;

---

[1] H. Treitschke, *Deutsche Geschichte im 19. Jahrhundert*, vol. iii. (1885), pp. 720-1 ; F. Engels, *Ludwig Feuerbach, und der Ausgang der klassischen deutschen Philosophie* (Stuttgart, 1888).

for both recognize that the formula of the identity
of the rational and the real could be invoked
equally by all political opinions and parties, which
differ from one another, not as to this common
formula, but in determining what is the rational
and real, and what the irrational and unreal: on
every occasion that a political party prepared for
war against an institution or class of society, it proclaimed its adversary irrational, *i.e.* devoid of solid
and real existence; and by this declaration brought
itself into line with Hegelian philosophy.   All
the wings of the Hegelian school variously
participated in the revolution of the nineteenth
century, and especially in that of 1848.   It was
even two Hegelians who wrote in that year the
vigorous *Communist Manifesto*.   But the formula
common to all of them was not an empty label;
it stood for the fact that the Jacobinism and the
crude naturalism of the century of the " Enlighten-
ment" were henceforth ended, and that all men
of all parties had learned from Hegel the meaning
of true political sense.   The early work, in which,
examining the condition of Germany, he defined
it as an " abstract state" (*ein Gedankenstaat*), has
reminded one of his critics of the Florentine
Secretary and his profound analysis of the
actual conditions of the Italy of the Renais-

sance.[1] And Cavour and Bismarck seemed to appear as splendid embodiments of the Hegelian theory, men in whom the rational and the real were always fused and united, in whom they were not estranged from one another, in the painful and futile conflict, characteristic of the minds of idealizers and dreamers.

The consequence to which this mediation of opposites led, combined with the destruction of false distincts and opposites, was the exaltation of history.   History—the life of the human race, facts which are developed in time—ceases to be conceived as something separate from and in-different to the essence of things, to the idea, or, what is even worse, as something which weakens and degrades the idea.   Thus had history appeared in the various dualistic systems ; not to speak of materialism, which, since it denies all values, cannot admit the value even of history.   And between historians and philosophers there had sprung up a profound disagreement, a mutual misunderstanding.   This is not the place to recall the most ancient forms of this disagreement, such as the philosophy of Descartes, which is pre-eminently antihistorical ; and Spinozism (or Oriental pantheism, as Hegel called it, adding

[1] Cf. K. Fischer, *Hegels Leben u. Werke*, p. 59.

that it was erroneously considered to be atheism, but should rather be called " acosmism "), and all the sensationalism and intellectualism of the eighteenth century. But even among Hegel's own contemporaries, history has no place in the system of Herbart, who is altogether without the idea of development ; nor in that of Schopenhauer, for whom the life of the human race does not present problems of progress ; nor in the positivist systems of Comte and of Spencer.

In the system of Hegel, on the contrary, where the infinite and the finite are fused in one, and good and evil constitute a single process, history is the very reality of the idea, spirit is nothing outside its historical development ; in it, every fact, precisely because it is a fact, is a fact of the idea and belongs to the concrete organic whole of the idea. For Hegel, therefore, *all history becomes sacred history.* On this point, too, it may be said that in a certain sense there is general agreement ; because particular attention and admiration has always been accorded to the great historical works, which were inspired by the influence of Hegel ; histories of religions, of languages, of literatures, of rights, of economics, and of philosophy. But Hegel's influence in historical studies has been generally considered

an accident, due simply to the personality of the
master, who was a passionate student and a con-
summate master of historical knowledge.   It was
not observed that it was really the inevitable
consequence of that much combated dialectic
principle of the solution of opposites and of false
opposites; or of the Hegelian logic in its most
characteristic aspect.   Thus the advancement of
historical study was recognized as a great benefit,
but the true reason of the advancement was
ignored; the consequence was accepted, the premiss was rejected.

The sacred character, assumed by history,
is an aspect of the character of immanence,
proper to Hegelian thought, to his negation of
all transcendence.   Certainly, it has been equally
an error to praise or to blame his thought as
materialism and naturalism; for how could a
philosophy, which reveals the genesis of these
illusions, a philosophy of activity, a philosophy
whose principle is spirit and idea, ever be
naturalistic and materialistic?   But when these
words were intended to signify the antireligious
character of Hegelian thought, there was some
truth in the observation.   It is a philosophy (I
should say the only philosophy), which is radically
irreligious, because it is not content to oppose

itself to religion or to range it alongside of itself, but it resolves religion into itself and substitutes itself for it. And for this same reason, from another point of view, it may be called the only philosophy that is supremely religious; since its task is to satisfy in a rational manner the need for religion — the highest of all man's needs. Outside of reason it leaves nothing; there is no insoluble remainder. " The questions to which philosophy has no answer have their answer in this, *that they ought not to be asked*."

The perpetual youth of the Hegelian philosophy, its indomitable vigour, its unexhausted fecundity lie, then, in the logical doctrine, and in the thought effectively in conformity with that doctrine. And its vigour, fecundity, and youth are increasingly apparent even in our own day, which is marked by a new efflorescence of neurotic mysticism, and of insincere religiosity, by an anti-historical barbarism engendered by positivism, and the Jacobinism which frequently ensues in these conditions. Whoever feels the dignity of man and the dignity of thought can find satisfaction in no other solution of conflicts and of dualisms than in the dialectical, the solution won by the genius of Hegel.

The one philosopher, who more than others

can be ranged with Hegel in this respect, is
G. B. Vico, whom I have already referred to as
the precursor of the antischolastic logical doctrine,
an æsthetician like Hegel, a preromantic, as
Hegel was a romantic, yet resembling him closely
in his genuinely dialectic thinking. Certainly
the attitude of Vico toward religion is less radical
than that of the later German philosopher. For
if Hegel, biographically speaking, was a very
ambiguous Christian, insufficiently explicit in
stating his position towards the Church, Vico,
from the biographical point of view, was a most
sincere and unequivocal Catholic. Nevertheless,
the whole thought of Vico is not only anticatholic,
but antireligious. For he explains how myths
and religions are formed by a natural process ;
and his renunciation of this principle of explanation in the single case of Hebrew history and
religion, if, from the subjective point of view,
it be the idiosyncrasy of a believer, objectively it
assumes the value of unconscious irony, similar
to the conscious irony of Machiavelli, when he
forbore to enquire how the Papal States ever
subsisted beneath a very bad government, because
(he said) "they are ruled by superior reasons,
to which the human mind cannot attain." Vico
establishes that the true is identical with the

deed, that only he who has done a thing can truly know it. Consequently he assigns to man full consciousness of the world of man, because it is his own work; and to God he restores knowledge of all the rest of the natural world, because he alone, who made it, has knowledge of it : a limitation, which forms but a slight obstacle to the revolutionary principle which he enunciated, and which, once established for the human world, must of necessity be extended to the whole of reality. And so profoundly irreligious was the whole theory of knowledge of this pious Catholic, that immediately after his death it was said that he had been obliged to conceal part of the thought in his books, by order of the churchmen. Rationalists saw in Vico their master, while zealous Catholics reproved him as the fountain-head of the antireligious movement of the historical epoch, which followed upon his.

But the resemblances between Vico and Hegel are far more evident when we leave this point of religion. As Hegel was in opposition to and in conflict with the antihistoricism of the Encyclopaedists and of the *Aufklärung*, so was Vico against the antihistoricism of Descartes and his school. He showed that if philosophers did not bring their reasonings into line with the

authority of philologists, and if philologists failed
to criticize their authority by the reasonings
of philosophers, both equally achieved only half
their purpose. As Hegel set himself in opposition to the Utopian preachers of abstractions
and champions of sentiment and enjoyment, so
Vico refuted at once both Stoics and Epicureans,
and recognized only those whom he called
"political philosophers." He railed at those
learned men who, forgetting the struggles and the
pains of which the web of reality is woven, dictated
"rules for conduct, impossible or dangerous to
the human condition, such as the regulation of the
duties of life by the pleasures of the senses";
and who gave laws and founded republics "in
shady repose," which "had no other habitation
than in the minds of the learned." He knew
well that "governments must conform to the
nature of the governed"; and that "native
customs, and above all the customs of natural
liberty, cannot be changed in a trice, but only
gradually, in the passage of time." Vico, not
less than Hegel, had the idea of the "*cunning of
reason.*" He called it *divine Providence* : " which,
out of the passions of men, all intent upon their
private advantage, for the sake of which they
lived like wild beasts in solitudes, has created

civil order, by which men live in human society."
What does it matter that men are unconscious
of what they do? The fact is not thereby the
less rational. "*Homo non intelligendo fit omnia,*
. . . because by understanding man explains his
mind and understands things, but when he does
not understand he creates things of himself, and
in so doing becomes that into which he transforms
himself." "And must we not say" (he exclaims
elsewhere) "that this is a counsel of superhuman
wisdom? Without the force of laws . . . but
making use precisely of the customs of men, of
those habits which are as unrestrained as the
natural expressions of human nature, . . . it
divinely regulates and guides them. It is true
that men have made for themselves this world
of nations; . . . but the profounder truth is that
this world is certainly the outcome of a mind
often different from, sometimes opposed, and
always superior to those particular ends, which
men had proposed to themselves. These narrow
ends, transformed into means for realizing wider
ends, this greater mind has always adopted in
order to preserve the race of man upon the earth.
Thus, for example, men wish to give free course
to their lusts and to abandon their offspring, and
thereby they create the chastity of marriage,

whence families arise; heads of families wish to exercise to the extreme their paternal power over their dependants, and thereby cities arise. The reigning classes of nobles desire to abuse their feudal power over the plebeians, and thereby they are brought into subjection to the laws, created by popular freedom; free peoples wish to loose themselves from the restraint of their laws and thereby they become subject to monarchs. Monarchs wish to strengthen their own positions by debasing their subjects with all the vices of dissoluteness, and thereby they reduce them to endure slavery from stronger nations; nations wish to destroy themselves, and by going into solitude to preserve what remains of themselves, whence, like the phœnix, they arise again. It was Mind that achieved all this, for there was intelligence in the actions of men. It was not Fate, for there was choice in their actions; nor Chance, for there was continuity; always from the same actions there followed the same results." [1]

These are the same ideas, often with the same metaphors, images, and turns of phrase as in Hegel. And this is the more wonderful, since

---

[1] The quotations from Vico are in the *Works*, ed. Ferrari, v. 96, 97, 98, 117, 136, 143, 146-7, 183, 571-2; vi. 235. [See now my *Philosophy of G. B. Vico*, Bari, 1911.]

the German philosopher (at least during the period that he was meditating his philosophy and composing his *Phenomenology of Spirit*) does not seem to have known the other "phenomenology," meditated in Naples a century earlier, under the title of *The New Science*. It almost seems as if the soul of the Italian Catholic philosopher had migrated into the German thinker, reappearing in him, at the distance of a century, more mature and more self-conscious.

THE CONNEXION OF DISTINCTS AND THE FALSE APPLICATION OF THE DIALECTIC FORM

How then has it come about that this system of philosophical thought, established with such logical depth, so rich in irresistible truth, so harmonious with and sympathetic towards concreteness, passion, fancy, and history, has appeared to some thinkers and has been condemned by them as abstract, intellectualistic, full of arbitrariness and artifice, at variance with history, nature, and poetry, in a word as the opposite of what it means to be? How can we explain the violent reaction against it, a reaction which seemed successful and definitive, and which it would be superficial (and little in the spirit of Hegel) to explain as entirely due to accidental motives, to lack of intelligence and to ignorance? On the other hand, how has it come about that this philosophical system has been invoked in support of the most different schools, such as materialism and theism, the very schools which Hegel intended to combat and to surpass? And how comes it too (if I may be permitted a personal instance, which perhaps does not relate exclusively to a personal case) that I, who am writing now with such a feeling of complete agreement, this interpretation of and commentary on the Hegelian doctrine of the synthesis of opposites, should for several years of my mental life have felt a marked repugnance to the system of Hegel, especially as it is presented in the *Encyclopaedia*, with its tripartite division into Logic, Philosophy of Nature and Philosophy of Spirit, both as I understood it myself, and as I saw it expounded and advocated by Hegelians? And how comes it that even now, in re-reading those works, I sometimes feel the old Adam, the old repugnance, arising within me?—The inmost reason for all this must be sought. Now that we have indicated the healthy part of the system, we must point out the diseased part as well. After having shown what is *living* in the system of Hegel, we must show also what is *dead* in it, the unburied bones, which hinder the very life of the living.

And we must not be too easily contented with

a concession, which has often been offered by
strictly orthodox Hegelians—the recognition that
Hegel could and did err in many of his statements of historical fact and of the natural and
mathematical sciences, owing to the limitations
both of the general state of knowledge of his
time and of his own individual culture. Such
Hegelians admit all this part of the system
must be re-examined and corrected, or even
reconstructed from top to bottom, in the light
of the progress of those special branches of
study. The implication would be that it is
only as historian and as naturalist that Hegel
is deficient and out of date; as philosopher, as
one who never founds his truth upon empirical
data, he remains intact. His adversaries rightly
remain unsatisfied with this concession; because
the source of the dissatisfaction with the system
of Hegel is not the quantity or the quality of
the erudition which it contains (most admirable,
despite its deficiencies and occasional archaisms),
but precisely the philosophy. I have declined
above to consider the influence of Hegel's
thought upon historical studies as something
separate from and independent of the principles
of his system. Here, for the same reason, I
cannot consent to consider the cause of his

errors as independent of his philosophical principles. Those of his errors which have seemed historical and naturalistic, are at bottom, or for the most part, philosophical errors, because they spring from his thought, from his method of conceiving history and natural science. Hegel is all of a piece; and it is to his credit that his errors cannot in general be explained as an accidental series of inconsequent irrelevancies.

The problem, then, is to seek out what might be the philosophical error or errors (or the fundamental error, and the others derived from it) which fused and combined in Hegel's thought with his immortal discovery, and thereby to understand the reaction against the Hegelian system, in so far as this reaction was not the usual obstructionism, which all original truths encounter, but rested on evidently rational grounds. And since, according to what has already been said, the logic of philosophy was the special field of Hegel's mental activity, it is to be presumed that there we shall find the origin of the error, which would in that case be an error of logical theory.

It is therefore a just feeling of the direction in which this search should be conducted that has led anti-Hegelian criticism in general to neglect the particular and incidental details of the system, and to set itself to exhibit the error of the principle of the synthesis of opposites itself, on the ground, either that the two terms are not opposed, or that their synthesis is not logical, or that it destroys the principle of identity and contradiction, or on similar grounds. Yet we have seen that substantially none of these objections is well founded, and every other objection that can be thought out satisfactorily proves to be equally unfounded : for that principle resists and will resist every examination and assault. The error of Hegel, then, is to be sought in his logic ; but, as it seems to me, in another part of his logic.

In the rapid summary of the various Hegelian doctrines given at the beginning of this work, when it was important to go directly to the problem of the dialectic, only passing reference was made to the doctrine of the relation of *distincts*, or, as it would be expressed in naturalistic logic, to the theory of classification. That doctrine must now be considered more closely, because it is my firm conviction that in it is hidden the logical error committed by Hegel, so weighty in its consequences.

The philosophical concept, the concrete universal or the Idea, is the synthesis of distincts, just as it is the synthesis of opposites. We talk, for example, of spirit, or of spiritual activity in general; but we also talk continually of the particular forms of this spiritual activity. And while we consider all of these particular forms essential to complete spiritual achievement (so that deficiency in any one of them offends us and impels us to find a remedy, and its total or partial absence shocks us as something monstrous and absurd), we are also jealous and vigilant that no one of them should be confused with any other. Therefore we reprove him who judges art by moral criteria, or morality by artistic criteria, or truth by utilitarian criteria, and so on. Even if we were to forget the distinction, a glance at life would remind us of it : for life shows the spheres of economic, of scientific, and of moral activity almost externally distinct, and makes the same man appear a specialist, now as poet, now as man of business, now as statesman, now as philosopher. And philosophy itself should remind us of the distinction, for it is not capable of expression without specialization into æsthetic, logic, ethic, and the like : all of them philosophy, yet each of them a philosophy distinct from the others.

These distincts, of which we have given examples and which are at once unity and distinction, constitute a connexion or a rhythm, which the ordinary theory of classification is not capable of explaining. Hegel saw this very clearly; and he never ceased to combat the importation of empirical classification into philosophy, the conception of concepts as subordinate and co-ordinate. In ordinary classification one concept is taken as foundation; then another concept is introduced, extraneous to the first, and this is assumed as the basis of division, like the knife with which one cuts a cake (the first concept) into so many little pieces, which remain separate one from another. With such procedure, and with such a result, farewell to the unity of the universal. Reality breaks up into a number of elements, external and indifferent to one another: philosophy, the thinking of unity, is rendered impossible.

Hegel's abhorrence of this method of classification caused him to reject prior to Herbart (incorrectly credited with the first statement of this criticism) the conception of faculties of the soul, to which Kant still adhered; and to reject (as he writes in 1802 [1]) that psychology which represents the spirit as a "bag full of faculties." "The feeling that we have of the living unity of the spirit," he repeats in the *Encyclopaedia* (§ 379, and cfr. § 445), and in all his other books, in the most various forms and on the most various occasions, "is itself opposed to the breaking up of the spirit into different forces, faculties, or activities, whatever they be, conceived as independent of one another." And be it observed that Hegel, always *sollicitus servandi unitatem spiritus*, was able to develop this criticism with far greater right and with far greater consistency than Herbart, who never succeeded in making his refutation of faculties of the soul agree with his atomistic metaphysic, and with his ethic and æsthetic, which consisted of catalogues of ideas, separated from one another and without relation to each other. But nevertheless, in the opinion of the writers of psychological manuals and histories of philosophy, Herbart passes for a revolutionary in his view of the spirit, and Hegel almost as a reactionary, who should have preserved the old scholastic divisions!

[1] *Verhältnis d. Skeptizismus zur Philosophie* (in *Werke*, xvi. 130).

If "distinct" concepts cannot be posited in separation but must be unified in their distinction, the logical theory of these distincts will not be the theory of classification, but that of *implication*. The concept will not be cut in pieces by an external force, but will divide itself by a movement internal to itself, and throughout these acts of self-distinction it will maintain its own identity; the distincts will not be in a relation of mutual indifference, but of lower and higher degree. The classification of reality must be replaced by the conception of degrees of Spirit, or in general of reality : the *classificatory* scheme by the scheme of *degrees*.

And the thought of Hegel set out on this path, the only one that conformed to the principle with which he started, the concrete universal. The theory of degrees permeates all his works, although it nowhere receives full and explicitly reasoned statement. Here, too, he had his precursors, whom we should investigate; and here, too, the philosopher most nearly akin to him is perhaps Vico. For Vico never distinguished spirit, languages, governments, rights, customs, religions, otherwise than as a series of degrees : spirit as *sense, imagination*, and *mind*; languages as *divine mental language, heroic* language, and language for *articulate speech* : governments as *theocratic*, *aristocratic*, and *democratic* ; rights as *divine* right, established by the gods, *heroic* right, established by force, and *human* right, established by fully developed human reason ; and so on. For this reason, Vico too conceived philosophy, not as a cabinet with separate pigeon-holes, but as "*eternal ideal history*, upon which particular histories appear in time." But if Hegel did not know the work of Vico, he had other incentives toward the solution which he sought. The very sensualism of the eighteenth century, especially the doctrine of Condillac, notwithstanding the poverty of its categories and of its presuppositions, seemed to him valuable, in so far as it contained the attempt to render comprehensible the variety of forms in the unity of spirit, by demonstrating their genesis. His criticism of Kant for having simply enumerated the faculties and the categories in his tables was supplemented by his appreciation of Fichte, for having affirmed the necessity of the "deduction" of the categories. But his true and proper precursor was Schelling's system of identity, with the method of potentiality, for which reality developed itself as a series of *powers* or degrees. "The subject-object" (thus did Schelling himself recall his juvenile conception in his vindication of himself against Hegel) "in virtue of its own nature, objectifies itself, but from every objectification it returns victorious and shows itself on every occasion at a higher power of subjectivity, until, when it has exhausted every one of its virtualities, it appears as subject triumphing over all." [1]

What does the theory of degrees mean? What are its terms, and what is their relation? What difference does it present to the terms and relation of the theory of opposites? In the theory of degrees, every concept—and let the concept be *a*—is both distinct from and united to the concept *b*, which is superior to it in degree; hence (beginning the exposition of the relation) if *a* be posited without *b*, *b* cannot be posited without *a*. Again, taking as an example the relation of two concepts, a case which I have studied at length elsewhere,[2] that of art and philosophy (or of poetry and prose, of language and logic, of intuition and thought, and so on), we see how an insoluble puzzle and enigma for empirical and classificatory logic resolves itself naturally in speculative logic, thanks to the doctrine of degrees. It is not possible to posit

---

[1] In the preface to the *Fragments* of Cousin.
[2] In my *Æsthetic as Science of Expression and General Linguistic.*

art and philosophy as two distinct and co-ordinate
species of a genus (which might be *e.g.* the
cognitive form) to which both are subordinate,
so that the presence of the one excludes the
other, as in the case of co-ordinate members.
There is proof of this in the many distinctions
between poetry and prose, which have been
given, and continue to be given, all of them most
vain, since they are founded upon arbitrary
characteristics. But the knot is unravelled, when
we think of the relation as one of distinction and
union together : poetry can exist without prose
(although it does not exclude it), but prose can
never exist without poetry ; art does not include
philosophy, but philosophy directly includes art.
And in fact, no philosophy ever exists save in
words, images, metaphors, forms of speech,
symbols, which are its artistic side, a side so real
and indispensable that, were it wanting, philosophy itself would be wanting. An unexpressed
philosophy is not conceivable : man thinks in
speech. The same thing can be proved by
adducing other dyads of philosophic concepts,
the transition from *rights* to *morality*, or from
the *perceptive* consciousness to the *legislative*
consciousness. Thus the real, which is one, is
divided in itself, grows on itself, to use the words

of Aristotle, or, to use those of Vico, passes
through its ideal history—and in the last stage,
which gathers up in itself all the preceding,
attains to itself, in its complete or perfect form.

If now we pass from the relation of the stages
a and b (in the example chosen, art and
philosophy) and pass to the relation of the
opposites in the synthesis, a, β, γ (employing
the example of being, not-being, and becoming),
we shall be able to perceive the logical difference
between the two relations. a and b are two
concepts, the second of which would be abstract
and arbitrary without the first, but which, in
its connexion with the first, is as real and
concrete as it is. On the other hand, a and β,
taken out of relation to γ, are not two concepts,
but two abstractions; the only concrete concept
is γ, becoming. If we apply arithmetical symbols
to the two connexions, we have in the first a dyad,
in the second a unity, or, if we prefer it, a triad,
which is triunity. If we wish to give the name
(objective) dialectic both to the synthesis of
opposites and to the connexion of the different
degrees, we must not lose sight of the fact that
the one dialectic has a different process from
that of the other. If we wish to apply to both
connexions the Hegelian terms " moments " and

"overcoming," which is at once "suppressing"
and "maintaining," we must note that these
terms bear different meanings in the two cases.
Indeed, in the theory of degrees, both the
moments are concrete, as has been noted; in the
synthesis of opposites both are abstract, pure
being and not-being. In the nexus of degrees *a*
is overcome in *b*, that is to say, as independent
it is suppressed and preserved as dependent:
spirit in passing from art to philosophy negates
art and at the same time maintains it as the
expressive form of philosophy. In the nexus
of opposites, considered objectively, *a* and *β*, in
their mutual distinction, are both of them
suppressed and maintained; but only meta-
phorically, because they never exist as *a* and *β*
distinct from one another.

These are profound differences, which do not
permit that both modes of connexion should be
treated in the same manner. The *true* is not in
the same relation to the *false* as it is to the *good*;
nor is the *beautiful* to the *ugly* in the same
relation as it is to *philosophic truth*. Life without death and death without life are two opposed
falsities, whose truth is life, which is a nexus of
life and death, of itself and of its opposite. But
truth without goodness and goodness without

truth are not two falsities, which are annulled in a third term : they are false conceptions, which resolve themselves in a connexion of degrees, for which truth and goodness are at once distinct and united : goodness without truth is impossible, since it is impossible to will the good without thinking it ; truth without goodness is possible, only in the sense in which that proposition co-incides with the philosophic thesis of the priority of the theoretic over the practical spirit, with the theorems of the autonomy of art and the autonomy of science.

Without doubt, *a*, being a concrete concept, that is, presenting the concrete concept in one of its particularizations, is also a synthesis of affirmation and negation, of being and not-being. Thus, to return again to the same ex-ample, artistic fancy lives as fancy ; and therefore it is concrete, it is activity which affirms itself against passivity, beauty which affirms itself against ugliness. And being and not-being become particularized, consequently, as truth and falsity, beauty and ugliness, goodness and wickedness, and so on. But this contest does not take place *for one degree in relation to another*; for those degrees, considered in their distinction, are the concept of the spirit in its determinations,

and not the universal concept of spirit considered
in its dialectic of synthesis of opposites. The
organism is the struggle of life against death ;
but the members of the organism are not therefore
at strife with one another, hand against foot, or
eye against hand. Spirit is development, history,
and therefore both being and not-being, becoming ; but spirit *sub specie aeterni*, which
philosophy considers, is *eternal ideal history*,
which is not in time. It is the series of the
eternal forms of that coming into being and
passing away, which, as Hegel said, itself never
comes into being and never passes away. This
is an essential point : if neglected we fall into
the equivocation, to which Lotze (alluding perhaps to a passage of the *Parmenides*) referred
when he wrote, that because the servant takes
care of his master's boots it does not follow that
the concept of servant takes care of the boots
of the concept of master !

When we say that the spirit is not satisfied
with art, and is driven by its dissatisfaction to
elevate itself to philosophy, we speak correctly ;
only we must not allow ourselves to be misled
by a metaphor. The spirit, which is no longer
satisfied with artistic contemplation, is no longer
the artistic spirit, it is already beyond that level

—it is the incipient philosophic spirit. And in the same way the spirit which feels itself dissatisfied with the universality of philosophy and thirsts for intuition and for life, is no longer the philosophical but the æsthetic spirit, a single and determinate æsthetic spirit which begins to fall in love again with some determinate vision and intuition. In the second, as in the first case, the antithesis does not arise in the bosom of the degree that has been surpassed. As philosophy does not contradict itself as philosophy, so art does not contradict itself as art; and every one knows the complete satisfaction, the profound and untroubled pleasure, which springs from the enjoyment of the work of art. The individual spirit passes from art to philosophy and passes again from philosophy to art, in the same way that it passes from one form of art to another, or from one problem of philosophy to another: that is, not through contradictions intrinsic to each of these forms in distinction from the others, but through the contradiction that is inherent in the real, which is becoming. And the universal spirit passes from *a* to *b*, and from *b* to *a* through no other necessity than that of its own eternal nature, which is to be both art and philosophy, theory and praxis, or however otherwise it may

determine itself. So true is this that if this
ideal transition were caused by a contradiction
which revealed itself as intrinsic to any determinate degree, it would no longer be possible to
return to that degree, which had been recognized
as self-contradictory : to return to it would be a
degeneration or a retrogression. And who would
ever dare to consider it a retrogression to return
from philosophy to æsthetic contemplation ? Who
could ever judge to be contradictory or erroneous
either of the essential forms of the human spirit ?
That transition of ideal history is not a transition,
or rather it is an *eternal transition*, which, from
this view-point of eternity, is a *being*.

Hegel did not make this most important distinction, which I have endeavoured to make
clear, between the theory of opposites and theory
of distincts. He *conceived the connexion of these
degrees dialectically, in the manner of the dialectic
of opposites*; and he applied to this connexion the
triadic form, which is proper to the synthesis of
opposites. The theory of distincts and the theory
of opposites became for him one and the same.
And it was almost inevitable that this should be
so, owing to the peculiar psychological condition
in which the discoverer of a new aspect of the
real finds himself (in this case, the synthesis of

opposites).   He is so tyrannized over by his own
discovery, so inebriated with the new wine of
that truth, as to see it everywhere before him,
and to be led to conceive everything according
to the new formula.   It was also almost inevitable that this should be so, owing to the relations,
close as they are subtle, which unite the theory
of distincts to that of opposites, and both to the
theory of the concrete universal or idea.   There
are also in the theory of degrees, as in that of
opposites, various moments that are overcome,
that is, are negated, and at the same time maintained : in the former too, as in the latter, there
is unity in diversity.   To discern the differences
between the two theories was reserved for a later
historical period, when the new wine was matured
and settled.

We can find proofs of the lack of this
distinction and of the confusion caused by its
absence at every step in the system of Hegel,
in which the relation of distinct concepts is
always presented as a relation of thesis,
antithesis, and synthesis.   Thus we find in the
anthropology : natural soul, thesis ; sensitive
soul, antithesis ; real soul, synthesis.   In the
psychology : theoretic spirit, thesis ; practical
spirit, antithesis ; free spirit, synthesis ; and

again: intuition, thesis; representation, antithesis; ethicity, synthesis; or again, in this
last: the family, thesis; civil society, antithesis; the state, synthesis. In the sphere of
absolute spirit: art is thesis; religion, antithesis; philosophy, synthesis; or in that of
subjective logic: concept is thesis; judgment,
antithesis; syllogism, synthesis; and in the
logic of the idea: life is thesis; knowledge,
antithesis; absolute idea, synthesis. And so
on. This is the *first case of that abuse of
the triadic form* which has offended and still
offends so seriously all who approach the system
of Hegel, and has been justly described as
an abuse. For who could ever persuade himself that religion is the not-being of art, and
that art and religion are two abstractions which
possess truth only in philosophy, the synthesis
of both; or that the practical spirit is the
negation of the theoretical, that representation
is the negation of intuition, civil society the
negation of the family, and morality the negation
of rights; and that all these concepts are
unthinkable outside their synthesis,—free spirit,
thought, the state, ethicity,—in the same way
as being and not-being, which are true only
in becoming? Certainly Hegel was not always

faithful to the triadic form (and indeed he declared in one of his juvenile essays that *quadratum est lex naturae, triangulum mentis*); and often, in developing particular cases, he minimized the error of the triadic form; but no such particular determination can suppress the principle of division assumed as foundation. On other occasions the triadic form seems almost to be an imaginative mode of expressing thoughts, which of themselves do not attain to their substantial truth. But to accept such an interpretation would be tantamount to discrediting that form in its logical value, *i.e.* in precisely the value which it must most fully maintain in the dialectic or synthesis of opposites. On the other hand, to defend the affirmations of Hegel with extrinsic arguments would be to proceed like an advocate who wishes to win with ingenuity rather than with truth; or like a swindler who puts forward money of good alloy, in order to pass false money in the confusion.

The error is not such as can be corrected incidentally, nor is it an error of diction: it is an essential error, which however small it may seem in the summary formula in which it has been given—the confusion between the

theory of distincts and the theory of opposites,—
yet produces the gravest results; that is to
say, from it arises, if I am not mistaken, all
that is philosophically erroneous in the system
of Hegel. This we must now examine in
detail.

V

THE METAMORPHOSIS OF ERRORS INTO PARTICULAR CONCEPTS AND DEGREES OF TRUTH (STRUCTURE OF THE LOGIC)

THE application of the dialectic of opposites to the relation of distincts, carried out with full logical seriousness (as indeed was to be expected from the vigorous and systematic mind of Hegel), was bound to entail, as it did, a double consequence. On the one hand, what are *philosophical errors* came to acquire the dignity of partial or particular concepts, that is, of *distinct concepts*; and on the other, what are really *distinct concepts* were lowered to the level of simple attempts at truth, to incomplete and imperfect truths: that is to say, they assumed the aspect of *philosophical errors*.

The first of these consequences determined the structure of the Logic, as we find it, at least in germ, in the *Phenomenology of Spirit*, and as it is set forth later in detail in the great *Science of Logic* (1812-1816), and in the small one of the *Encyclopaedia* (1817, 1827, 1830). The second determined the character of æsthetic and gave origin to the two philosophical sciences of history and of nature, as they may be seen, chiefly in the *Encyclopaedia*, and in the courses of lectures posthumously published.

To begin with the first point, opposites and distincts being confused with one another, the abstract moments of the concept (which in its truth and concreteness is the synthesis of opposites) are naturally taken to be related to one another in the same way that the lower concepts are to the higher. For example, being and nothing, which in relation to becoming are two abstractions, become, by analogy, two degrees, in the sense in which, for example, in the series of distinct concepts, intuition, thought, and practical activity, intuition and thought are stages relative to the third stage, practical activity. But what are those two abstractions, *being* and *nothing*, taken separately, each in itself, but two falsities, or two errors? Indeed, the first of these corresponds for Hegel to the Eleatic or to other allied philosophical views, which conceive the absolute as simple *being*, and God as nothing but the whole of all reality, the most real. The second corresponds to the Buddhistic view, which conceives nothingness as the base of things, as the true absolute. They are therefore two opposite, yet similar, philosophical errors, both of which claim to think the indeterminate and abstract as supreme reality. And what, on the other hand, are *intuition* and *thought* but two truths? The first term sums up the whole imaginative activity of man and gives rise to a particular philosophical science, —Æsthetic; the second is the crown of all human scientific activity and gives rise to the science of sciences—Logic. They are, therefore, not two unreal abstractions, but two concrete and real concepts.

Once this has been posited, it becomes clear that owing to the confusion between the dialectic of opposites and the connexion of distincts and to the assumption that the opposites, taken abstractly, fulfil the same function as the distinct concepts, those errors become transmuted into truths. They become particular truths, truths of a lower degree of spirit, but still necessary forms of spirit, or categories. And when these errors have been baptized truths of a certain kind, there is nothing to hinder every error, error in general, being considered particular truths. *The phenomenology of error thus assumes the appearance of an ideal history of truth.*

This baptism, this transfiguration, has seemed, and will still seem to some, to be the recognition of a principle as important as it is profound. Do we not frequently speak, even in ordinary language, of progressive errors, of errors which open the way to truth? Do we not say that humanity has learned more from certain errors than from many truths? The Eleatics were wrong in conceiving the absolute as simple being; but that error of theirs nevertheless affirms an undeniable, though partial truth, that the absolute is also being. Descartes and Spinoza were wrong in positing the parallelism of mind and body, of thought and extension; but unless, thanks to that very error, the distinction between the two terms had been fixed and thrown into relief, how could their concrete unity have been thought afterwards? Kant was wrong in presenting the antinomies as insoluble; but it was thus he came to recognize the necessity of the antinomies, the

basis of the dialectic. Schelling was wrong
in conceiving the absolute as simple identity;
but that error of his was the bridge which had
to be crossed to reach the conception of the
absolute as unity in opposition and distinction.
Unless Plato had conceived the Ideas as
transcendent, how could the merely logical
concept of Socrates ever have been changed
into the Aristotelian concrete (συνόλου)? How
could the *a priori* synthesis of Kant ever have
appeared without the sceptical negation of
Hume? He who wishes truth to be generated
without error wishes for the son without the
father. He who despises error despises truth
itself, for truth is incomprehensible without
those antecedent errors, which are therefore
its eternal aspects.

But here too we must be careful not to
allow ourselves to be led astray by metaphors;
we must re-think the thing itself. In
error, that which may justly be called progressive, or fruitful, or the like, is not error but
truth. When we consider a doctrine as a
whole, we may declare it to be false or true;
but if we consider it more in detail, the doctrine
resolves itself into a series of affirmations,
some of which are true and some false; and

its progressiveness and fruitfulness lie in the
affirmations which are true, not in those which
are false, and which therefore cannot even be
called affirmations.   Thus,   in   the   Eleatic
doctrine, the affirmation that the absolute is
being, is true : what is false, is that it is nothing
but being.   Even in the highest expression of
truth, " The absolute is spirit," the absolute
is being, though not simple being.   Similarly,
in the Cartesian and Spinozist parallelism, the
distinction of mind from body, of thought from
extension, is, at least in a certain sense, true ;
but it remains to be explained how it is
produced : what is false is the hasty metaphysical
theory, which explains those two terms by
making them two manifestations of God, or
two attributes of substance, and takes the
statement of the problem for the solution.
Thus too, in Platonic transcendency, the truth
lies in the value assigned to the idea, as no
longer purely subjective, but as objective and
real : the error lies in separating the ideas
from real things, and in placing them in a
world which we cannot think, but can only
imagine ; and in thus imagining them we
confuse them again with things real and finite.
It is the error in each of these doctrines that

is the incentive to progress : it is the not-being, the necessary moment of development ; without contradiction and doubt, without perplexity and dissatisfaction, we should make no advance. Man would not conquer truth, because he would cease to think, and indeed would altogether cease to be. So much we know henceforth : it is the principle of the synthesis of opposites, which has been. expounded and fully accepted above. But if this principle affirm the synthesis of being and not-being, *it does not therefore possess the virtue of changing not-being into being*, darkness into light, the incentive to progress into progress, error into partial truth or degree of truth. The error, which is preserved in truth as a particular degree or aspect of it, is that aspect of truth which is contained in the doctrines that we call erroneous. These aspects of the truth are the true subject of the history of thought : error as error is the hemisphere of darkness, which the light of truth has not yet illuminated ; and we write the history of successive illumina- tions, not of darkness, which is without history, because it accompanies every history. Therefore the transmutation of errors into truths, this first consequence of the transference of the dialectic of opposites to the connexion of distincts, into which Hegel allowed himself to be drawn, is to be considered as fundamentally erroneous.

If these explanations, which I have premised, and if these canons of judgment which I have laid down, be exact, we are now in a position to understand the problem and the structure of the Hegelian *Logic* : not indeed, be it well understood, the principle of the logical doctrines of Hegel (the concrete concept) and of his various particular doctrines (the theory of opposites, the theory of distincts, etc.)—of which we have already discoursed in preceding chapters—but of that determinate thought which led Hegel to conceive a fundamental science, which he called *Logic* or *the Science of logic*, and developed in three sections, the logic of *Being*, the logic of *Essence*, and the logic of the *Concept*. It is a science, which has, not without reason, seemed strange and obscure, rigorous in appearance, but arbitrary in fact and at every step ; something unseizable, because it provides no secure point to take hold of or to lean upon.

The problem of the Hegelian *Logic* (as appears from the principal content of that book) is to submit to examination the various definitions of

the Absolute, that is, to review critically all forms
of philosophy, in order to demonstrate, by means
of their difficulties and contradictions, the truth
of that philosophy which considers the Absolute
as spirit or idea. Further, it is to show at the
same time that the aspects of truth brought to
light by other philosophies find their justification
in this conception, so that this philosophy is the
result, as it has been the aspiration, of all the
efforts of human thought. Hence in the *Logic*
there pass before us, now sometimes expressly
named, now sometimes in allusion and reference,
Oriental Emanationism, Buddhism, Pythagorean-
ism, Eleaticism, Heracliteanism, the Atomism
of Democritus, Platonism, Aristotelianism, the
doctrines of the Pantheists, of the Sceptics and
of the Gnostics, Christianity, Saint Anselm,
Scholasticism; then, too, Descartes, Spinoza,
Locke, Leibniz, Wolff, Hume, Kant, Fichte,
Schelling, Jacobi, Herder; and other philosophical points of view. It is the "pathology of
thought," as it has been called by an English
writer, in a sense somewhat different from mine :
it is the polemic, by which every philosophy
affirms and maintains its life against other philosophies, more or less discordant with, and hostile
to it.

This polemic, if we observe it well, can be conducted in two distinct modes, one of which presupposes the other as its basis. The different philosophies, and their partially erroneous points of view, can be studied in their individuality, in the definite form that they assumed with various thinkers at different times, in chronological sequence; and we thus have the *History of Philosophy* (which is both history and criticism, like every true history). Or we can study the universal possibilities of philosophical errors, their perpetual sources, the confusion of philosophy with the various other activities of the human spirit; and in this case the polemic against errors is *philosophy itself*, the whole system; for it is only in the completely developed system that the causes of errors become clear. A polemic against errors can be placed, for convenience' sake, now at the beginning, now in the middle, and now at the end of a philosophic theory; but logically it is inseparable from the philosophy itself, because, as Bacon said, as the straight line is the measure both of itself and of the curve, so *verum index sui et falsi*; or, as is generally said, every affirmation is also negation. This criticism, which is the entire system, is also the basis of that other criticism, the history of philosophy.

Hegel, by the affirmative theses of his philosophy, discharged magnificently the task of criticizing philosophical errors : certainly, within the limits of his system, or up to the point at which the errors of his own system prevented him from seeing further into the errors of others ; but in any case with a breadth and richness such as no other philosopher, save Aristotle, had ever displayed. Aristotle indeed stands to the previous development of Hellenic thought in the same relation as Hegel stands to the whole philosophical development up to his own time, from the Hellenic, even from the Oriental world. Hence the *Logic* of Hegel has on several occasions been compared with and placed beside the *Metaphysic* of Aristotle.[1]

And for this reason, in the *History of Philosophy* also, Hegel attained to heights never reached previously to him and rarely since, so much so that he is considered as the true founder of the history of philosophy, no longer understood as literary history or as a collection of erudite matter, but as internal history, as an exposition which philosophy itself makes of its own genesis in time, as the great autobiography of philosophic thought.

---

[1] " C'est la seule métaphysique qui existe, avec celle d'Aristote. "   H. Taine, in a letter of 1851 : see *Sa Vie et sa correspondance* (Paris, 1902), i. 162-3, cf. p. 145.

But owing to the confusion between the dialectic and the connexion of distincts, and to the consequent conception of errors as particular truths, Hegel was not satisfied with the two modes indicated, but attempted a *third mode*—that realized in the structure of the *Logic*. Here errors are treated as distinct concepts, that is, as categories; and the attempt is made to deduce, or to develop errors, in the same way that the categories or the distinct concepts are deduced and developed. The method proper to truth is applied to non-truth.

What was bound to happen in this desperate attempt, this violent and spasmodic effort toward the impossible? "*S'il est difficile, c'est fait; s'il est impossible, on le fera*," said some courtier-minister of the *ancien régime*. And he performed the impossible with a fiat of his will, leading the state to ruin and provoking the revolution. Similarly his own will ruled supreme in the structure that Hegel devised. He begins at the beginning. Hegel always gave himself great trouble over this problem of the beginning, not less than over that of the *introduction* to be provided to philosophy (the senseless dispute as to the place that the *Phenomenology* has in the system is well known). Yet he himself recognizes quite clearly that philosophy is a "circle" and thereby implies the inconceivability of a necessary starting-point. A circle can be entered at any point; and so it is with philosophy. We can begin with the concept of spirit in general, proceeding from that by determinations, or we can proceed by successive complications from the most simple concept, or by discomposition, from the most complex, or from some intermediary concept, by going backwards and forwards; or, finally, from some problem and philosophical investigation and criticism of errors, we can work to a complete system. It is in this way that every one begins to philosophize; and here, at this point, is reality: each one has his beginning, τὸ πρῶτον πρὸς ἡμᾶς, and at this stage of apprehension there is no πρῶτον φύσει. The preference to be accorded to one beginning rather than to another is at most a question of didactic convenience. But if the problem of the beginning is of no importance in philosophy, it is true, on the other hand, that philosophy, objectively considered, has its first position, its πρῶτον φύσει: a first, which is also last, the first which is a circle, such as, for example, in the philosophy of Hegel, Spirit or Idea. But in the *Logic*, in so far as it is an examination of a series of errors, how can a first

be thought that should be first of necessity, a
πρῶτον φύσει? Hegel began with pure being,
that is, with the examination of the philosophical
systems which define the Absolute as simple
being; and he repeatedly tried to justify this
beginning, but in vain. It was a beginning like
any other, equally justified with any other; but
unjustifiable if it is claimed to justify it as the
only one. Why should we not commence with
the philosophies which place the root of things
in one of the other of the cosmological elements,
the water of Thales or the air of Anaximenes?
Or with the sensationalist philosophies, for which
the absolute is the relative, and reality is the
phenomenon? Let the starting-point be pure
being : only, an examination which begins at
this point, has "commanded" a principle, like
that laid down in the mathematical disciplines.
Or again, the course of the argument has a
purely biographical, autobiographical, or æsthetic
value. Indeed, the *Phenomenology*, which begins
from sensible certainty, and the *Logic*, which
begins from pure being, follow here and there a
course, which recalls some philosophic romance :
Émile, perhaps, or the journey of the Irishman
in search of the best of religions.

The beginning was arbitrary; and the sequel

was arbitrary.   It is not easy to hold Hegel's
Logic in one's mind, unless recourse be had to
learning it mechanically : for there is no necessary
generation of its successive parts from one another.
Triad follows triad ; but it does not appear that
one triad links itself to another, triadically, as
the method implies.   After the first triad, of being,
not-being, and becoming, comes the category .of
the determinate being (*Daseyn*) : but if there is
to be a link between them, determinate being
should arise from becoming as its antithesis, *i.e.*
as not-becoming.   But the fact is that Hegel
himself says, that determinate being corresponds
to pure being in the preceding triad.   For this
reason, the series of triads of the Hegelian *Logic*
has been interpreted by some critics, not as a
great uninterrupted chain, but as a single fundamental triad, into which other triads are inserted ;
and into which still others could be inserted, as
well as that limited number which Hegel gave,
apparently by way of example.   But on this
interpretation, the necessary ascent through
different degrees, from pure being to the idea,
is made illusory, and that ascent was the purpose
of the Logic.   So the book is thus reduced to a
congeries of criticisms directed against the affirmations of abstract terms, which are resolved in

dialectic syntheses. And it would be necessary to add that the criticisms are concerned not only with abstract opposites, but also with false opposites; and therefore it is not altogether an erroneous view which has noted a certain change of method in the *Logic*, as it gradually rises from the primary to the ulterior categories. It is clear that the content of the criticism changes, when we pass from the errors concerning being to those which refer to essence and to the concept; hence Hegel himself says, that "in being we have another and a passing into another; in essence, the appearing in the opposite, and in the concept, the distinction between the particular and universality, which continues as such in that which is distinct from it, and is in a relation of identity with the distinct."[1]

If there be no necessary connexion between the successive parts of Hegel's *Logic*, there appear in it on the other hand marks of the tendencies which might be expected in a thought-content, which has been compelled into those schematic forms, as into a bed of Procrustes. That content, as has already been said, could only be developed, either in the form of the exposition of a complete philosophic system (and

[1] *Enc.* § 240.

in this case, as a philosophy of spirit), or in the form of a history of philosophy. And the treatment of the *Logic* approximates sometimes to the one type, sometimes to the other. For instance, we discover an attempt at a history of philosophy in the order of the first categories, in which appear successively Parmenides, Heraclitus, Democritus; and then again, in other parts, Descartes, Spinoza, Kant: the first part of the doctrine of the concept contains the critique of the Aristotelian analytic; the second part, the criticism of the Leibnizian monadology. And again, it has an even stronger tendency to transform itself into a philosophy (speculative and not empirical) of spirit, *i.e.* of the particular forms of spirit, cognitive and practical, in their necessary relation. Thus, in the doctrine of being (section on quantity) there is the gnoseology of arithmetical procedure; in the doctrine of essence, of the theory involved in the natural sciences. In the doctrine of the concept, in the first section, there is the logic of the concept, of the judgment, and of the syllogism; and then, in the third section, the more properly philosophical logic. In the parts relating to objectivity, the concepts of mechanism and chemism are elucidated, and in those relating to teleology and life, there is a sketch of a philosophy of nature ; while a practical philosophy appears in the section on the Idea, in the discussion of will. Finally, æsthetic is not altogether excluded : in the compendium of logic, which is to be found in the *Propaedeutic* of 1808–1812, the category of the " Beautiful " is united to that of " Life." [1] For this reason also, it is desperate to attempt to keep the various parts of the system of Hegel distinct from one another. The *Logic* anticipates the *Philosophy of the Spirit*, which takes up again the themes of the *Logic*, the *Philosophy of nature* develops the doctrines of being and of the essence ; the parts of the *Logic* relating to mechanism, to chemism and to life, anticipate the *Philosophy of nature* : the *Phenomenology of Spirit* contains the whole system in a first sketch (if we do not take account of the *System der Sittlichkeit*, which Hegel did not publish, and which was the very first sketch).

A concrete content, taken from the history of philosophy, and in great measure from the Philosophy of spirit, a violent and arbitrary arrangement, imposed by the false idea of an *a priori* deduction of errors : that is how the Hegelian

---

[1] *Philosophische Propädeutik*, ed. Rosenkranz, 2nd course, § 10 (in Werke, xviii. 120).

Logic presents itself to me.   The arrangement
injures the content.   But in saying this and in
condemning the undertaking of Hegel, as em-
bodied in the *Logic*, I do not intend to condemn
to death and to oblivion that richest of all the
books which bear the title *Logic* ; on the contrary,
I mean to place it in conditions favourable to its
life and to the continued exercise of its profound
influence upon the mind.   He who takes up the
Logic of Hegel, with the intention of understanding its development and above all the reason of
the commencement, will be obliged ere long to
put down the book in despair of understanding
it, or persuaded that he finds himself face to face
with a mass of meaningless abstractions.   But he
who, like the dog of Rabelais, "a philosophical
beast," instead of leaving the bone alone, takes
a bite at it, now here and now there, chews it,
breaks it up and sucks it, will eventually nourish
himself with the substantial marrow.   Hegel and
his disciples after him, have persistently pointed
to the door by which the *Logic* can be entered :
pure *being*, from which we must gradually pass
by the vestibules and up the stairs of *nothing*,
of *becoming*, of *determinate* being, of *something*,
of the *limit*, of *change*, of *being for self*, etc. etc. :
in order to reach the sanctuary of the Goddess, or

the Idea.   But he who obstinately knocks at that
gate and believes the false information, that such
and no other must be the door and the stair, will
vainly attempt to enter the palace.   That door,
which has been indicated as the only one, is a
closed, indeed a sham door.   Take the palace by
assault from all sides ; thus alone will you reach
the interior, and penetrate to the very sanctuary.
And it may be that you will see the countenance
of the Goddess lit with a benevolent smile, be-
holding the " saintly simplicity " of many of her
devotees.

VI

THE METAMORPHOSIS OF PARTICULAR CONCEPTS INTO PHILOSOPHICAL ERRORS

I. ART AND LANGUAGE (ÆSTHETIC)

THE other consequence, the second counter-blow arising from the confusion between the synthesis of opposites and the relation of distincts, was not less grave. Owing to this confusion, Hegel deprived himself of the means of recognizing the autonomy and of attributing their just and proper value to the various forms of the spirit. Error was confused with particular truth, and, as philosophical errors had become for Hegel particular truths, so particular truths were bound to be associated with errors and to become philosophical errors, to lose all intrinsic measure, to be brought to the level of speculative truth, and to be treated as nothing but *imperfect forms of philosophy*.

For this reason, Hegel did not completely succeed in recognizing the nature of the æsthetic, or of the historical, or of the naturalistic activity ; that is to say, of art, or of history, or of the physical and natural sciences.

Without doubt, the pages of Hegel concerning æsthetic are animated with great artistic feeling ; and on the whole there prevails in them the tendency to make art a primary element in human life, a mode of knowledge and of spiritual elevation. We are carried by these pages far beyond and far above the vulgar view, for which art is a superfluous accident of real life, a pleasure, a game, a pastime ; or a simple mode of instruction, empirical and relative. The constant contact of Hegelian speculation with taste and with works of art, and the dignity which it assigned to the artistic activity, gave it an effective influence over men's minds and made it a powerful stimulus to the study of æsthetic problems. This is a merit, which, in part, is common to all the æsthetic theories of the Romantic period (the great period of the fermentation and the renewal of the philosophy of art and of literary and artistic criticism and history), and which, in part, is peculiar to the Hegelian æsthetic, in virtue of its wealth of ideas, of judgments and of problems.

But the elements of truth, scattered in plenty in the Hegelian æsthetic, are either too general, or merely incidental, and are, in principle, divergent from the fundamental concept of art, which Hegel accepts, and which is erroneous.

It is erroneous, because Hegel, firm in his belief that every form of spirit (save the ultimate and supreme form) is nothing but a provisional and contradictory way of conceiving the Absolute, could not discover that first ingenuous theoretic form, which is the lyric or the music of spirit, and in which there is nothing philosophically contradictory, because the philosophic problem has not yet emerged. This first form is its condition. It is the region of the intuition, of pure fancy, of language, in its essential character, as painting, music or song : in a word, it is the region of art. When Hegel begins his meditation upon the phases of spirit, he is already at a point where that region is behind him, and yet he does not recognize that he has passed it. The *Phenomenology* takes its start from *sensible certainty*, according to Hegel the simplest form of all : that in which (he says) we behave towards reality in an immediate or receptive manner changing nothing in it and abstaining from all the labour of concepts. And he does not find

it difficult to show that such contemplation, which
seems to be the richest and most true, is, on the
contrary, the most abstract and the poorest.
The thing is *now*, and is not the *moment after*;
it is *here*, and in a moment, in the *here* there is
something else; all that survives, is the abstract
this, *here*, *now*; everything else disappears. But
the sensible certainty, of which Hegel speaks, is
not the first theoretic form; it is not genuine
sensible certainty, αἴσθησις pure and simple. It
is not, as he believes, immediate consciousness:
it is already mingled with intellectual reflexion,
it already contains the question as to what is
truly real. In place of genuine *sensible certainty*
(such as we have in æsthetic contemplation,
where there is no distinction between subject
and object, no comparison of one thing to another,
no collocation in spatial and temporal series)
there has been substituted the *first reflexion* upon
sensible knowledge; and it is natural that that
first reflexion should seem imperfect and to be
surpassed. Hegel often repeats that: " the
subject without predicate resembles, in the
phenomenon, the thing without properties, the
thing - in - itself, an empty and indeterminate
foundation; it is the concept in itself, which, only
with the predicate, receives differentiation and

determination." But art is, precisely, subject without predicate; that is quite other than the nothingness and void of the thing-in-itself and of the thing without properties. It is intuition without intellectual relations; it is the emotion, which a poem communicates, through which there opens a view of a reality, which we cannot render in intellectual terms and which we possess only in singing or in re-singing, that is, only in creating it.

Since Hegel never reaches the region of æsthetic activity and therein the theoretic form which is truly primary, so he does not succeed in explaining language. Language, too, becomes, in his eyes, an organized contradiction. Indeed, for him it is the work of memory, which he calls "productive," because it produces "signs"; and the sign is explicitly defined as an immediate intuition, which represents a content "altogether different from that which is its own." By means of language the intelligence impresses its representation upon an external element. The form of language, therefore, is intellectual; it is the product of a logical instinct, which is afterwards theorized in grammar. Owing to this logical form, language tries to express the individual, but cannot do so: "you wish to say *this*

piece of paper, upon which I am writing, or rather
have written,—precisely *this*; but you do not say
it.   What you say is a universal, the *this*."
Thus, according to Hegel, does language confute
itself, attempting to express the individual, and,
on the contrary, always expressing the universal.
—But for the *omne individuum ineffabile* of the
scholastics, which Hegel here seems to repeat,
we must substitute the opposite *solum individuum
effabile* (or ·else correct the former with the
addition : *logicis modis ineffabile*).   How can we
ever think that a human activity, such as language,
does not attain its end, that it proposes to itself
an end that is absurd and therefore that it must
dwell in self-deception, from which it cannot
escape?   Language is essentially poetry and
art : by language, or by artistic expression, we
grasp individual reality, that individual shading,
which our spirit intuites and renders, not in terms
of concepts, but in sounds, tones, colours, lines,
and so on.   For this reason, language, understood in its true nature, and in the full extent of
its meaning, is adequate to reality.   The illusion
of inadequacy arises when the term language is
applied to a fragment of this full meaning, and
when that fragment is separated from the organic
whole to which it belongs.   Thus paper, this

paper, of which I speak, is not only what is expressed by the words "this paper" in themselves, torn asunder from their context and rendered abstract. It is what my eyes, or rather, my whole spirit, has present to it; which in so far as it represents, it can also render externally, with sound, colour, and so on. If I say: "this paper precisely," it is because I have it before me and am showing it to others: the words that issue from my mouth obtain their full meaning from the whole psychical situation in which I find myself, and so from the intention, intonation, and gesture, with which I pronounce them. If we abstract them from that situation, certainly they will appear inadequate to that individual: but that is because we have made them so, by mutilating them. But Hegel (who had no clear idea of the æsthetic condition of the spirit) could not completely understand language; he was obliged to think of it in that mutilated and intellectualized manner, and therefore to declare it contradictory. And when, in his *Æsthetic*, he passes from the language of prose to consider the language of poetry, he falls back into the old rhetoric, after some attempt to emerge from it. Poetic language also, in the end, he regards as a mere "sign," essentially different from the lines and the colours of sculpture and of painting, and from the tones of music.

Thus Hegel's erroneous logical theory concerning distinct concepts conceals from him the place that properly belongs to the æsthetic activity; and suggests to him a philosophy of language, which leads him of necessity to consider language as an error. But it is not only language that is treated in this fashion. Art, its true function unrecognized, obtrudes itself upon his mind; and since he does not know what to make of it, he transfers it to a place, where it does not belong and where, like language (which has first been arbitrarily separated from the representative and æsthetic activity, with which it altogether coincides), it too ends by appearing as nothing but imperfection and error. Hegel could neither pass it by in silence nor get rid of it lightly (as is the way of naturalistic and positivist philosophers). His time would not permit this, nor would his individual disposition, in which interest in art was so prominent. The conception to which he attained was substantially that of his time. Kant, in the third *Critique*, had studied the æsthetic activity along with the teleological judgment, as one of the modes of representing nature, when the mechanical conceptions of the exact sciences are surpassed; Schiller had indicated it as the ground of reconciliation in the struggle between necessity and liberty, and Schelling conceived it as the true organ of the Absolute.   Schopenhauer was later to consider it in like manner as the contemplation of the Ideas and the freeing of the will.   For Hegel also, this activity, which the whole romantic period sometimes substituted for, sometimes placed above, and sometimes placed below religion and philosophy, became a mode of apprehending the Absolute, of solving the great philosophical problem.   In the *Phenomenology*, he makes it a form of religion, superior to merely natural religion (which adores material objects, fetiches and the like), because it is indeed a mode of adoring spirit as subject; in the *Encyclopaedia* he makes it, with but slight difference, the religion of beauty, a first degree in relation to revealed religion, inferior to the latter, as this latter, in its turn, is inferior to philosophy.   The history of poetry and of art consequently appears in the lectures on *Æsthetic*, as a history of philosophy, of religion and of the moral life of humanity: a history of human ideals, in which the individuality of works of art, that is to say, the properly æsthetic form, occupies a secondary place, or is referred to only incidentally.

If the conception of art, as engaged upon the same problem as religion and philosophy, is common to his time, what is peculiar to Hegel is the relation which he establishes between those three forms : the distinctive character, which he assigns to art in relation to religion and philosophy. Hegel could not, as others did, make the æsthetic activity complementary to the philosophical activity, solving in its way the problems that were insoluble to philosophy.   Still less could he make it an activity superior to the philosophical.   His logical assumption was bound to lead him to the usual solution of the dialectic, in its application to distinct concepts.   The artistic activity is distinct from the philosophical only through its imperfection, only because it apprehends the Absolute in a sensible and immediate form, whereas philosophy apprehends it in the pure medium of thought. This means, logically, that art is not at all distinct ; and that for Hegel it is practically reduced (whether he like it or not) to a philosophical error, or an illusory philosophy.   True art would be philosophy, which addresses itself again to the same problem upon which art has worked in vain and attains a perfect solution of it.

That such is the genuine thought of Hegel, is proved by the fact that he does not shrink from the extreme consequence of this theory. When philosophy is completely developed, art must disappear, because it is superfluous: art must die, and indeed it is already quite dead. If it is an error, it is not necessary and eternal. The history of art, which Hegel traces, is directed to shewing the gradual dissolution of the artistic form, which has no place, in modern times, in our true and highest interests. It is a past, or the survival of the past. This grandiose paradox illuminates everywhere the æsthetic error of Hegel, and better perhaps than any other example makes clear the error of his logical assumption. In defence of Hegel, it has been said that the death of art, of which he speaks, is that eternal death, which is an eternal rebirth: such as we observe in the spirit of man, when he passes from poetry to philosophy, rising from the intuition to the universal, so that in his eyes, the world of intuition loses its colour. But against this interpretation, there is the fact that Hegel speaks of the death of art, not in the sense of perpetually renewing itself, but as actually about to happen and as having happened, of a *death of art in the historical world*. This is in complete agreement with his treatment of the degrees of reality as a series of opposites, difficult to abstract and to

separate from one another.   Once he had assumed
this application of the dialectic, Hegel had no
other choice than one of two ways, either to
suppress art by means of that grandiose paradox,
or to preserve it with a not less grandiose
inconsistency.

For this reason, it is not altogether wrongly
that the system of Hegel (whose twin principles
of the concrete concept and the dialectic, are of
frankly æsthetic inspiration) has appeared to be
a cold intellectualism, irreconcilable to the artistic
consciousness.   And the misunderstanding of
art leaves its traces in his treatment of all the
problems into which the concept of art enters as
a necessary and proximate premiss.   Hegel is
usually considered an adversary of the Aristotelian
formal logic; but it would be better to say, with
greater exactness, that he was the adversary of
classificatory and naturalistic logic, or, better still,
that he limited himself to revealing the inadequacy
of classificatory and naturalistic logic to provide
a principle for philosophy.   We have already
recognized this merit in him and his polemic
on this subject could not have a different meaning.   "Aristotle" (he says) "is the author of intellectual logic (the logic of the abstract intellect),
whose forms concern only the relation of finites

between themselves; the true, therefore, cannot be conceived in them."[1] But the method of classification is not what is most characteristic in the logic of Aristotle and of his school: the classificatory tendency is also to be found in the Baconian or inductive logic. The characteristic of the Aristotelian logic is its syllogistic, or verbalism, the confusion into which it falls between logical thought and speech, and its claim to establish logical forms, while limiting itself to verbal forms.

Hegel did not and could not criticize this error, because he was without the instrument of criticism, which can be furnished only by a valid philosophy of language. He certainly tries to distinguish between the proposition and the logical judgment; but he cannot adduce good reasons for this distinction, and he states that a proposition (for instance "it is hot") becomes a judgment only when with it we answer the doubt that may arise as to the truth of the affirmation. The exact distinction was beyond his reach, for it consists in recognizing that the pure proposition is nothing but speech itself, or language as pure æsthetic fact, in which there is no logic, though it is the necessary vehicle

[1] *Gesch. der Philos.*[2] ii. 365-68.

of logical thought.   Indeed, not only does he retain the tripartition of concept, logical judgment
and syllogism, and the division between elementary forms and methodology, between definition,
division, demonstration and proof, but he even
sets to work to distinguish and define new classes
of judgments and of syllogisms.

VII

THE METAMORPHOSIS OF PARTI-
CULAR CONCEPTS INTO PHILO-
SOPHICAL ERRORS

II. History (Idea of a Philosophy of History)

It might be said that the failure to understand
the autonomy of art also prevented Hegel from
understanding the character of history (historiography). But the truth is that Hegel was unable
to do full justice to this theoretic form, for the
same reason as in the case of the others, *i.e.* as
we have already mentioned, because he transformed particular concepts into philosophical
errors. From the logical point of view, the two
errors have the same origin. Psychologically, it is
probable that the first prepared the way for the
second; as it is also psychologically probable
that Hegel's idea of religion contributed in some
measure to produce the first. He regarded
religion as an imaginative and more or less

imperfect form of philosophy; and this was
bound to lead him to assign an analogous position
to art in relation to philosophy.

History, herein differing from art, presupposes
philosophical thought as its condition; but, like
art, it finds its material in the intuitive element.
History, therefore, is always narration, and never
theory and system, though it has theory and system
at its foundation. So that, on the one hand,
historians are trained to the scrupulous study of
documents, and on the other to the formation of
clear ideas upon reality and life, and especially
upon those aspects of life which they undertake
to treat historically. It has seemed therefore
that history cannot dispense with scientific
accuracy and yet remain always a work of art.
If all historical works be reduced to their simplest
expression, the historical judgment, or the proposition affirming that " something has happened "
(for example, Caesar was killed, Alaric devastated
Rome, Dante composed the *Comedy*, etc.), we
see, upon analysing these propositions, that each
one of them is constituted of intuitive elements,
which act as subject and of logical elements,
which act as predicate. The first for instance
and speaking generally, will be Caesar, Rome,
Dante, the *Comedy*, and so on; and the second,

the concepts of slaughter, devastation, artistic composition, and such like.

From this historical gnoseology, it follows that every progress of philosophic thought is translated into a progress of historical knowledge, since we understand far more adequately what were truly the historical facts of Dante's composition of his poem, when we know better what poetry and artistic creation are. But we also gather that the attempt would be vain to resolve those historical affirmations into abstract philosophic affirmations. That would be to absorb the whole and complete fact in what is merely the condition of the fact. History can give rise to a conceptual science of an empirical character, as when we pass from it to a sociology that proceeds by types and classes; but for that very reason, it is not absorbed by that conceptual science, of which it remains the presupposition or the basis. Conversely, history can give rise to philosophy, when we pass from the historical consideration of the particular to the theoretical elements, which are at the bottom of that consideration; but, for that very reason, it cannot be said to be absorbed in that philosophy, which is its pre-supposition and its basis. A *philosophy of history*, understood not as the elaboration of this abstract philosophy, but as *history of a second degree*, a history obtained by means of that abstract philosophy, is a contradiction in terms.

What is the significance of such an idea of a philosophy of history, as history of a second degree? Neither more nor less than the annulment of history. For this second degree, this postulated philosophical consideration of historical narrative, this philosophic history, would be true history, in relation to which the history of the historians would be revealed as error, because it is constructed according to a method which does not lead to truth, or, what amounts to the same thing, does not lead to complete truth. On the appearance of the second form, the first form would be dissolved; or rather, it would be dissolved, precisely because it would not be a form, but something formless. The idea of a philosophy of history is the non-recognition of the autonomy of historiography, to the advantage of abstract philosophy. Whenever such a claim is made, one seems to hear the bells tolling for the death of the history of historians. The historians —usually so docile when their attention is called to some progress in science or philosophy, which may help to make clear some part of their work as narrators—yet rebel with violence when any one talks to them of a philosophy of history, of some sort of speculative method of knowing history, or when the attempt is made to persuade them to consign the labour, into which they have put all their powers, and of which every line and every shade is dear to them, to the hands of philosophers who are not historians, to revise and complete it. And their rebellion is reasonable. It is just as if a painter or a musician were told to consign to the philosophers his picture or his score, when he had completed it, so that they might raise it to the second power, by introducing into it strokes of the philosophic brush and philosophic harmonies.

Hegel had to posit and did posit the idea of a philosophy of history; and he had to negate, as he did negate, the history of the historians, for that was required by his logical presupposition. He divided philosophy into *pure* or *formal* philosophy (which should have been logic, and was also metaphysics), and into *applied* and *concrete* philosophy, comprising the two philosophies of nature and of spirit, into the second of which the philosophy of history entered again; the three together composed the encyclopaedia of the philosophical sciences. Thus Hegel adopted as his own the traditional Scholastic division of

philosophy into *rational* and *real*, and this not as
a simple formula and external scheme, but as
expressing also the demand for a philosophic
treatment of the contingent facts of nature and
of human history. All history, as I have previously explained, can be called concrete or
applied philosophy; but these words did not
possess so innocent a meaning for Hegel as for
ourselves. For him they implied the sharp distinction of the history, contained in the philosophical encyclopaedia, from all the other histories,
which constitute the work of historians. In his
lectures upon the philosophy of history, this distinction is very clearly drawn, for he places on
the one side *original* historiography and *reflective*
historiography (the second of these two being
subdivided into general, pragmatic, critical and
conceptual history), and on the other *philosophic*
historiography or *philosophy of history*.

Hegel affirms that this philosophic historiography should have its own method, different
from the method of ordinary historiography, and
he claims for it the character of an *a priori* construction. It is true that by this he sometimes
seems to mean, not a distinctive character, but
only the need for a better elaborated *a priori*.
He notes that ordinary historians also write

a priori history, for they proceed from certain thoughts and representations of their own, which, though defective and arbitrary, yet are always *a priori*. But the *a priori* that he introduces is not the logical element, the interpretation of intuitive data, which has been recognized above as indispensable for all historical work. Rather, it is a *history already complete*, which needs only to be clothed in names and dates. " The one thought " (writes Hegel) " with which philosophy approaches history is the simple thought of reason : that reason rules the world, and therefore in the history of the world also, there is a rational process." But there is far more in it than this, or rather, we learn what these words really mean, when we see him trace the necessary process of reason in the historical world. The history of the world is the progress in the consciousness of liberty : its single moments or degrees are the various national spirits (*Volksgeister*), the various peoples, each one of which is destined to re-present one degree only, and to accomplish only one task in the whole achievement. Before Hegel seeks the data of facts, he knows what they must be ; he knows them in anticipation, as we know philosophic truths, which spirit finds in its own universal being and does not deduce from contingent facts. In the *History of Philo-sophy*, which is perhaps his principal historical work, he knows *a priori* that the history of philosophy and the system of philosophy are identical. The theme is the same development, which is represented in the system itself in the pure medium of thought, free from historical externalities; and in the history it has the addition of these externalities (names and dates). The first phases of Hellenic thought are the first categories of metaphysic and the phases follow one another in the same order as the categories.

Against an interpretation of Hegel's theory of the philosophy of history, might be set his various declarations of the great respect due to actual fact. But we must first examine what value these declarations can assume or retain. "That there is rational process in the history of the world" (he says) "should be shown by the con-sideration of history itself . . . it should be a result: we must take history as it is, and proceed historically and empirically." The accidental is extraneous to philosophy; and history (he says elsewhere) "should lower the universal into empirical individuality and into effectual reality; the idea is its essence but the appearance of the idea is in the sphere of accident and in the realm

of arbitrary choice." But if accident and individuality are truly extraneous to philosophy,
if we can know them only empirically, there can
be no *a priori* philosophy of history, but only
history itself. And if a philosophy of history be
created, then this accidental and individual, and
the historical and empirical method, are not
recognized and are refuted. We cannot escape
from the dilemma. To recommend attention to
facts, or to recognize that the study of documents
is the indispensable point of departure for history,
are mere words, when in consequence of the
adoption of certain principles, it is not known
what use to make of those facts and documents.
Those of Hegel's disciples, who have believed
that they could save both the goat and the
cabbage by maintaining both the speculative and
the philological methods in history, have saved
neither the one nor the other. It is very
ingenuous to affirm that one and the same
activity can be exercised with two different
methods; for the method is intrinsic to the
activity, and a duplicity of methods means a
duplicity of activity. It is worse than ingenuous
to make the two methods alternate and come to
one another's assistance, as though they were two
friends and companions engaged in the same task.

At other times, Hegel seems to understand his *a priori* scheme as nothing but a rough anticipation of what is given by actual history: "It may be thought" (he writes in the *History of Philosophy*) "that the philosophic order of the degrees of the idea must be different from that of the concepts which are produced in time ; but in the *Whole* (*im Ganzen*) the order is the same." At other times again he modifies his statement in such a way that hardly anything remains of it. Thus, in affirming the identity of the philosophic system and the history of philosophy, he observes : "The philosophy which is last in time is also the result of all preceding philosophies, and should contain the principle of them all : it is therefore—*but only if it be truly a philosophy*— the most developed, the richest and the most concrete." The reservation implied in the parenthesis amounts to a tautological affirmation, that the most developed, the richest and most concrete philosophy, is not the last in time, but that which is truly a philosophy ; since it is possible that a philosophic system which constitutes a regression may appear last in time. What are we to conclude from all this? That Hegel never had in mind an *a priori* philosophy of history, the idea of which is, however, closely

connected with his dialectic treatment of distincts?
No, but rather that error is contradiction; and
that Hegel's erroneous thesis of a philosophy
of history (of an *ideal history*, which is not *eternal*,
but *in time*) shows itself to be error, by the
involuntary contradictions in which Hegel becomes involved.   Certainly, we cannot conclude
that those admissions suffice to heal the defects of
the erroneous thesis and to change it into truth.

That the philosophy of history, thus conceived,
should not suffer beside itself history properly
so-called, but should negate it, is not merely a
probable inference, from Hegel's principle, but is
explicitly enough stated in several propositions.
And indeed, the very fact that he defines the
philosophy of history as "the *thinking* contemplation of history" (recalling immediately afterwards, that thought alone distinguishes man
from the animal), is confirmation that he regards
history as such, either as not thought, or as
imperfect thought.   And the attitude of antipathy
and depreciation, which he adopts toward professional historians, is likewise significant; almost
as though a philosopher of art should quarrel
with professional poets and painters.   But most
instructive of all is what he says of the facts
which are the material of the historian's study.

The only facts which, in his opinion, are valuable
for history are those which represent the movement of spirit or the history of the State. All the
particular facts that remain " are a superfluous
mass which, when faithfully collected, only oppress
and obscure the objects worthy of history ; the
essential characteristic of the spirit and of the
times is always contained in great events. It
is, therefore, a true sentiment that has led to
the handing over of such representations of the
particular to romances (such as those of the celebrated Walter Scott, etc.). It is to be held a
proof of good taste to unite pictures of unessential and particular life to a subject-matter equally
unessential, such as those that fiction extracts
from private facts and subjective passions. But
to mingle, in the interests of so-called truth,
individual trivialities of time and people with the
representation of general interests is not only
contrary to judgment and to taste, but contrary
to the concept of *objective truth*. For, according
to this concept, the truth for spirit is that which
is substantial, not the vacuity of external existence,
and of accident. It is perfectly indifferent whether
such insignificant things are formally documented,
or, as in fiction, invented in a characteristic
manner and attributed to such and such a name,

or to such and such circumstances." Whoever
meditates these words will find in them most
plainly the pernicious distinction between two
kinds of facts, between historical facts and non-
historical facts, essential facts and unessential facts,
which has often since reappeared among the disciples of Hegel. It reappeared first in Edward
Gans, who, when publishing the lectures of the master
upon the philosophy of history, took occasion to
repeat that this discipline would lose in dignity if
it had to encumber itself with the micrology of
facts, and that consequently its function was to
demonstrate the necessity, not of all facts, but
only of the great epochs of history and of great
groups of people, and to leave the rest to merely
narrative history. And it has reappeared right
down to that Italian Hegelian, who maintained
some years ago, in a well-known polemic, that
documents were necessary, to establish in what
prisons Thomas Campanella was successively
confined, and how many days and hours he
suffered torture : but were not necessary for the
determination of the historical meaning of his
thought and action. This second thing would
be deduced *a priori* from the ideas of the
Renaissance, the Catholic Church, the reforms
of Luther, and the Council of Trent. Such dis-

tinctions, so far from preserving a class of facts as necessary for true history, make it that *all facts, even the very notion of fact, are rejected as useless.*   Indeed, what reason is there for regarding the facts *a, b, c, d, e* as unessential and superfluous, other than that they are individual and contingent?   And are not the facts *f, g, h, i, k, l,* which it is wished to declare essential and indispensable, equally contingent and individual?   If it be a contingent fact that Napoleon suffered from cancer of the stomach, will not the 18th Brumaire and the battle of Waterloo be also contingent?   Will not the whole epoch of the Revolution and the Empire be contingent?   And thus (since individuality and contingency extend to all facts), the whole history of the world will be contingent.   And, on the other hand, if the French Revolution and the 18th Brumaire and Waterloo were necessary facts, we do not see how necessity can be denied to Bonaparte, who was an actor in the drama; and to Bonaparte just as he was constituted in effective reality: in his strength and in his mental and physical weaknesses; in his resistance to fatigue in his early years, which enabled him to remain whole days erect on horseback and to spend whole nights bent over his little table of work, and in

the abdominal disease of his mature years.   As
reality has neither kernel nor shell and comes
forth all in a jet, as the internal and the external
are all one (and Hegel has taught this), so the
mass of facts is a compact mass, it is not composed
of an essential kernel and an inessential shell, of
facts that are intrinsically necessary and facts that
are superfluous externalities.   When these distinctions are adopted in ordinary language, there is
always implied a reference to definite historical
representations, in relation to the theme of which,
and only in relation to that definite theme, certain
masses of facts appear superfluous.   The distinction is so evidently relative that, if we change
our point of view, and pass from one theme to
another, what before was superfluous becomes
necessary, and what before was necessary becomes
superfluous.

But in the passage quoted there is one thing
more to be noted.   Hegel hands over to romance,
that is, to a form of art, the facts which do not
seem to him to be historical—we should say
all facts ; and since art was for him a provisional form, which philosophy dissipates and
displaces, this is another way of shewing the evil
fate of history at the hands of Hegelian philosophy.
It is a strange fate that the same philosophy,

which, in virtue of one of its logical doctrines, had so effectively vindicated the value of history, of the *res gestae*, found, as the result of another of its logical doctrines, that it could not recognize the value of the *historia rerum gestarum* and so of the same *res gestae*. Famished for history, nourished on history, Hegel's philosophy, without understanding that it did so, yet advocated fasting. And the contradiction blazed in the light of the sun, before the eyes of all the world; for, as there issued from the school of Hegel a series of great writers of history, so there came forth from the same school the most petulant and comic depreciators of history and of fact that the world has ever seen.

VIII

THE METAMORPHOSIS OF PARTICU-LAR CONCEPTS INTO PHILO-SOPHICAL ERRORS

III. Nature (Idea of a Philosophy of Nature)

It was certainly a more difficult task to understand the true limits, or the true nature, of the natural and mathematical disciplines. From the Renaissance onward, there had taken place a continual enlargement of what was called experimental and mathematical science, the *exact science* of nature ; and science had come more and more to rule the intellect, even life itself. Philosophical speculation gave way before exact science, or received to some extent its imprint, as is plain from many parts of the systems of Descartes, Spinoza, and Leibniz. The sensationalism and materialism of the eighteenth century had been the ultimate consequence of that predominance of the naturalistic ideal.

It is true that when the mind of Hegel was
forming, a movement of doubt and of reaction
had already commenced, and (not to speak of
Vico, who must again be mentioned here) it
was being made clear in several quarters of
Germany that exact natural science was inadequate to attain to real reality, to the bottom
of things. Philosophers like Kant, armed at all
points with mathematics and with empirical
knowledge, analysing the methods of the exact
sciences and drawing their conclusions, proclaimed
the limits of scientific knowledge, and assigned
the fundamental problems to the practical reason
and to æsthetic and teleological intuition.   Other
philosophers, like Jacobi, studying the most
notable monument of the application of exact
science to speculative problems, the philosophy
of Spinoza, showed that with the method of the
finite sciences we cannot escape from the finite,
and therefore declared that God and the infinite
and moral problems belonged to the realm of
feeling and of immediate knowledge.   Poets,
artists and men of letters, at the time of the
Sturm und Drang, felt the cold and the void
of the intellectualism of the *Aufklärung*; and
like Goethe, they aspired to a vision of a
living nature, to be revealed only to him

who should contemplate it with a sympathetic soul.

Hegel accepted this critical inheritance, and gave it vigorous expression, by establishing, as has already been mentioned, the difference between the method of philosophy and that of the mathematical and natural disciplines.

Nevertheless, even in this movement which seems so hostile to the ideal of the exact sciences, the weight and power of that ideal makes itself an effective influence. For example, if Kant deny to exact science the possibility of solving the fundamental problems, it is also certain that, for him, the only science to which man can attain is just this exact science; and the solutions which he proposes by another method, have not cognitive or thought value for him; that is, they have not true value. If Jacobi criticize the method of the finite sciences in relation to the knowledge of God, it is none the less certain that, for him, the only form of knowledge is that of the finite sciences; the other is not knowledge, it is not translatable into the form of thought, and remains "sentiment."

In Hegel and in his immediate predecessor Schelling, things would seem to take a different form, because both posited as true knowledge the knowledge of the intellectual intuition and of the idea. But, on deeper investigation, we discover in both the same prepossession (which could be called the specially modern prepossession), in favour of the exact sciences, though in them it receives a new statement. Instead of excluding the exact sciences from philosophy, and of considering philosophy as incapable of scientific exactitude, Schelling and Hegel *consider the exact sciences as insufficiently scientific and include them in philosophy, which elaborates them, rendering them scientifically rigorous and supplying them with an internal necessity.* Kant and Jacobi, each in his own way, made the exact sciences non-philosophical in character, and philosophy non-scientific; Schelling and Hegel make the exact sciences a semi-philosophy, and philosophy the true science. These are two different solutions of a problem, but for both the same assumptions. And the principal of these is the persuasion that the exact sciences have theoretic value, or that their concepts are more or less perfect logical formulations.

Now, in order definitely to settle the dispute between exact science and philosophy, and to recognize the respective rights of both, it was necessary to adopt an altogether different method.

So long as the naturalistic and philosophic
methods were taken to be two methods of
scientific truth, conflict was inevitable, for the
reason already recorded, that a determinate
activity has but one intrinsic method, its own.
Hence, if the first method were admitted to be
science, the second was shaken and was bound
to fall ; philosophy had to be eliminated. Conversely, if the speculative method were admitted
to be the only method of truth, the other was a
mere clumsy and contradictory tentative on the
lines of the first method and had to yield before the
complete development of the speculative method.
The mathematical and naturalistic disciplines had
to be replaced by philosophy, since they were a
mediocre philosophy, which could not maintain
itself against a better philosophy. On the other
hand, the way of escape, taken by Kant and by
Jacobi, the consigning of philosophy to the
practical reason or to sentiment, *i.e.* to the non-
theoretical, was closed, once thought had been
shewn capable of the solution of the problems of
reality, and philosophical logic had been discovered. The only other way that was open
was to consign the naturalistic and mathematical
disciplines, *i.e.* exact science, to the non-theoretical,
that is, to the practical. This path has been

entered upon in our day, and it seems to me that
it must increasingly appear, not only fruitful, but
necessary.

It cannot be said that Hegel had no notion of
the practical nature of the naturalistic and mathematical disciplines.   His books are rich in analysis
and observations, which could be transplanted
without alteration into the books of the most
modern theorists of the method of those disciplines.
Read his pages on the concept of *law* in the
empirical sciences.   Law (he says) is nothing but
the constant image of the inconstant appearance ;
so that, in passing from the more particular to
the more general laws, in reducing them to unity,
we run into tautologies, in which the intellect
expresses not the reality of things, but only its
own necessity.   What is the postulate, that in a
uniformly accelerated movement, the velocities
are proportionate to the times, but just the
definition of a uniformly accelerated movement ?
And what are the numerous hypotheses worked
out by the physicists but assertions, which correspond neither to empirical reality nor to the
philosophic concept, as, for example, the pores, of
which we speak, without their being demonstrated
by experience ?   Of the notion of centrifugal and
centripetal forces, Hegel observes that it is a

metaphysical monster, which is simply presupposed and which we are forbidden to submit to
any intellectual examination as to the mysterious
fashion in which it happens that these forces
increase and decrease and each in turn acquires
or loses its preponderance.   In the exact sciences,
what is called thinkable is unthinkable, because
it is false.   " It is quite *thinkable*, as they say,
that a uniformly increasing and decreasing movement should take place in circles ; but this *think-
ability* is nothing but an abstract possibility of
representation, which neglects the determinate
character of what is under consideration, and
which therefore is not only superficial, but false."
In the same way, in mathematics, the name
irrational is applied only to what the science
contains of reality and *rationality*.

In addition to these and to very many other
similar observations, which are scattered in
profusion, both through the *Phenomenology* and
the *Logic*, as well as through the *Philosophy of
Nature*, there recur frequently in the pages of
Hegel the words *intellectual fictions* (*Verstandes-
fiktionen*), *arbitrary conceptions* (*willkürlich*), to
indicate the constructions of the abstract intellect
and of the natural and mathematical disciplines.
And fiction and arbitrariness appeal precisely to

the voluntary and practical activity; and since
those acts of will have a secular history and are
the result of most noble efforts and are held in
high esteem, even in enthusiastic admiration, on
account of the proved utility of the results
attained, it should be evident that it was impossible to speak of acts of will in a depreciatory
sense, or of practical acts, as if these were performed at the bidding of caprice and of evil
passions; but rather in the sense of acts of will
rationally justifiable or of legitimate practical acts.

But there is a case in which Hegel explicitly
shows that he recognizes the non-scientific, yet
legitimate character of those constructions, as
they are and as they must remain. It is where
he propounds to himself the question as to
whether *philosophic mathematics* are possible:
that is, "a science which knows by concepts
what ordinary mathematical science deduces from
presupposed determinations according to the
method of the intellect." His answer is that
such a science is impossible. "Mathematics"
(he says) "is the science of the finite determinations of magnitude, which must remain and
have value in their finitude and must not pass
beyond it; and therefore it is essentially a science
of the intellect. Since it has the capacity of

being a perfect intellectual science, it is desirable
rather to preserve to it the advantage which it
possesses over other sciences of the same kind,
than to disturb it by the admixture of the concept, which is heterogeneous to it, or of empirical
ends" (*Enc.* § 259). "If we desired to treat
philosophically the configurations of space or of
unity" (he had said in the preceding edition of
the same book), "they would lose their meaning
and their particular form: a philosophy of them
would become a matter of logic or of some other
concrete philosophical science, according as a
more concrete meaning came to be attributed to
the concepts." He knew, on the other hand,
that "arithmetic does not contemplate numbers
and their figures, but *operates* (*operiert*) with them;
for number is indifferent determinateness and
inert, and must be set in motion and placed in
relations, from without." Once a form of activity
was admitted, which operates with thought-data
but does not think them, there should have been
no difficulty in extending the observation and in
attaching to it all the other scattered observations
on the non-theoretical procedure of the natural
and mathematical disciplines, and thereby attaining a truer theory of the genuine nature of exact
science.

Hegel also had very clearly in mind a concept of *nature*, or of the *naturalistic method*, not metaphysical, but simply gnoseological, *i.e.* a method applicable not only to the so-called inferior manifestations of reality (the three natural kingdoms), but also to all the others (to the *orbis intellectualis*). Thus he considered Hugo Grotius's theory of the external right of States as analogous to the natural philosophy of Newton : Aristotelian logic seemed to him to be nothing but a *naturalistic science* of thought, in which the forms of thought were described and placed alongside one another, as is done in natural history with the unicorn and the mammoth, with the black-beetle and the mollusc; and the same comparison was suggested in ethics by the doctrine of virtue (*Tugendlehre*). By this path, too, he should have been able to reach the conclusion that the content of the so-called natural sciences is not indeed a part of reality, but a mode of treating all reality, a mode which arises and persists side by side with the philosophical, precisely because, confined within its own limits, it does not compete with philosophy.

Another characteristic observation of Hegel, which would lead to the same result, is the affirmation, upon which he greatly insists, that nature, herein differing from humanity, *has no history*. Now, if all reality be movement and development, how can a part of reality ever be conceived, which is not, together with the whole, in process of becoming? But, in truth, that which has no history is *nature in the naturalistic sense*; that is to say, nature contracted and mummified in abstract classes and concepts. And this affords another ground against considering these classes and concepts as modes of apprehending real reality. An English critic has opportunely noted that the philosophy of history, or the treatment of universal political history, corresponds, in the *Philosophy of the spirit*, to the section on objective spirit, in the same way that the histories of art, of religion and of philosophy, which Hegel has specially treated elsewhere, correspond respectively to the section on absolute spirit, which comprehends the three spheres of art, religion, and philosophy. Thus in that philosophy of spirit, only the section on subjective spirit or psychology has no corresponding historical treatment: no history is given of man, considered psychologically.[1] Why? Precisely because psychology is a naturalistic science and is thus condemned to the same historical

---

[1] Mackintosh, *Hegel and Hegelianism*, p. 236, n.

sterility which has been recognized in nature in general.

But notwithstanding these suggestions, notwithstanding the observations which he had occasion to make and the admissions which more or less consciously fell from his lips, Hegel did not draw the conclusion which seems to us correct. He did not proclaim the philosophical indifference of the natural and mathematical disciplines and their complete autonomy; he turned instead towards the solution which had already been adopted by Schelling, when he had conceived a *philosophy of nature*. The reason is quite clear. He was driven to that conclusion by his logical presupposition. As art and history had appeared to his mind as philosophical errors to be turned into truths, the one in pure philosophy, the other in the philosophy of history as he had conceived it; so analogically, the natural and mathematical disciplines could not retain their relative autonomy as practical formulations of reality and of experience, and had to be treated as philosophic attempts and partial errors, to be turned to truth in a philosophy of nature. " The antithesis " (he says) " between physics and philosophy of nature is not that between a not-thinking and a thinking of nature. A philosophy of nature means nothing

but a thinking contemplation of nature; and this
ordinary physics also is; for its determinations
of forces, laws, etc., are thoughts; only, in physics
those thoughts are formal and intellectualistic."
" In the philosophy of nature there is no other
question than just the replacing of the categories
of the intellect by the relations of the speculative
concept and the understanding and the determining of experience according to these relations."
Not only must philosophy agree with natural
experience; but the birth and formation of
philosophic science has empirical physics as
presupposition and condition." He well sees
that in the natural sciences, classifications are
purely artificial, and their purpose is to give
clear and simple marks as aids to subjective
knowledge; but he nevertheless believes that
they can be replaced by " natural " classifications,
and it seems to him that he has discovered a kind
of beginning of such classifications in the researches of comparative anatomy and in the
division of animals into vertebrate and inverte-
brate, and of plants into monocotyledons and
dicotyledons, and others similar to this. He
often speaks elsewhere of an " instinct of reason,"
which should manifest itself in the theories of the
physicists and naturalists, in which the speculative

concept would be in some measure anticipated.
And this explains also why he defends against
the naturalistic and mathematical nominalism of
Locke, the reality of natural genera and of
mathematical concepts, and why he preserves
unshaken his faith in the "eternal laws of nature."

A single remark suffices to show how unten-
able is this equivocal position.   If any one
wishes to apply philosophy to historical facts, he
cannot do otherwise than narrate history (which
in order to be history must always be to some
extent philosophically illuminated); and if any one,
in the presence of history, is seized with the
desire for a philosophical system, he cannot do
otherwise than abandon historical exposition and
expound abstract philosophy; so, in the same
way, if any one, in the presence of the natural
sciences, is disturbed by the need for philosophy, he has but two ways of satisfying it,
according as his need is for a concrete or for an
abstract philosophy.   In the first case, he must
pass from the natural and mathematical disciplines
(and from their intellectualist and arbitrary concepts) to the historical vision of the things of
nature and of man; in the second, he must
simply and solely return to philosophy.   But a
philosophy of nature, a philosophy which should

have the natural sciences as its *base*, is also (as, on another side, the *philosophy of history* is) a contradiction in terms; because it implies philosophic thought of those arbitrary concepts, which philosophy does not know, and upon which it consequently has no hold, either to affirm or to deny them.

Hegel repeatedly called attention to the difference between his philosophy of nature and Schelling's, criticizing the latter for being founded upon the analogy between organic and inorganic, upon the comparison of one sphere of nature with another, and developed by the application of a prearranged plan. But Hegel's philosophy of nature is equally incapable of development, save by means of *analogy*. The only difference is that in it the analogy is taken from the forms of the concept, and that he there talks of judgment, syllogism, dialectic opposites, and the like. Hence the divergence between the two philosophies, mother and daughter, has, in my opinion, but slight importance. Nor does it seem to me fitting to attribute to Hegel's natural philosophy, with its concept of becoming and of evolution, the merit of being the precursor of Darwin's discoveries. The evolution and the dialectic of the concepts, in Hegel's philosophy

of nature, is purely ideal.   It leaves natural
species intact, and indeed proclaims their fixity.
" It has been a clumsy representation on the
part of ancient as well as of modern philosophy
of nature, to regard the progress and transition
from one natural form or sphere to a higher
as an actual product of external reality, which,
in order that it may be made *clear*, has been
driven back into the *obscurity* of the past.   Externality is the special characteristic of nature,
by means of which she permits differences to
assert themselves and to appear as indifferent
existences : the dialectic concept, which guides
the degrees in their progress, is immanent in
them.   Nebulous representations, which are at
bottom of sensible origin, like those of the birth
of plants and of animals from water and of the
most highly developed animal organisms from
the lowest, etc., must be altogether excluded
from philosophic consideration " (*Enc.* § 249).
This is sheer hostility to the hypothesis of
transformation and it is what might be expected
from Hegel, who does not recognize any *historicity*
in nature.

Certainly, when we speak of the fallacious
idea of a philosophy of nature and condemn the
mode of treatment proposed by Hegel, it is not

necessary to include in the condemnation the whole book which bears that title. The devil is not so ugly as he is painted; and Hegel's book also contains (generally in observations appended to his paragraphs, these forming the greater part of the book) a host of most just criticisms, which seem at first glance to be directed against mathematicians, physicists and naturalists, but which are really directed against the metaphysic which they mingle with their teachings, or wrongfully deduce from them. That is to say, they are directed against the "ineffable metaphysic," as Hegel calls it, which changes into realities these mathematical and naturalistic abstractions, like forces, pores, atoms and so on. Here Hegel is quite right and we cannot withhold from him our lively agreement.

This polemic is also the only just part of the violent invective against Newton, or against the bad metaphysic, which Newton (although he had uttered the warning: "Physicists, beware of Metaphysic"), introduced or suggested. For the rest, the invectives of Hegel are documents of the hostility towards naturalists and mathematicians, which the idea of a philosophy of nature brought with it; just as the idea of a philosophy of history inspired a certain hostility

against professional historians. His hostility, as
we have said, did not arise from contempt for
those disciplines; it came rather from an excess
of love, from the too lofty and philosophical idea,
which Hegel still had of them and which made
him severe towards those who cultivated them.
Nevertheless, his *bête noire* was destined to
become the greatest representative of modern
exact science.   Hegel accumulated criticisms,
accusations and sarcasms against Newton, from
the dissertation *De orbitis planetarum* to the last
edition of the *Encyclopaedia*.   In the dissertation,
he deplores "*illam, quae Newtone incepta est,
mathematices et physices confusionem*"; and he
remarks jestingly about the little story of the
apple, that this fruit was three times fatal to the
human race, causing first the sin of Adam, then
the destruction of Troy, and finally by falling
upon the head of Newton, the ruin of natural
philosophy![1]   Newton (he says, summarizing, in
the *History of Philosophy*) was the chief contributor
to the introduction into science of the reflective
determinations of forces, by substituting the laws
of forces for the laws of phenomena.   In physics
and optics, he made bad observations and even

[1] . . . *universae generis humani, deinde Troiae miseriae principiis
pomum adfuisse, malum et jam scientiis philosophicis omen*" (in *Werke*,
xvi. 17).

worse syllogisms.   From experience he passed
to general points of view, made these fundamental,
and from them constructed single facts.   Such is
the nature of his theories.   He was a barbarian
in the use of concepts, and never bethought
himself that he was employing determinations of
thought.   He handled concepts as we handle
stones and pieces of wood.   The experiments
and reasonings of his Optics, which are adduced
as the most sublime example of such operations
in the study of nature, should really serve as an
example of how one should not experiment or
reason.   Nature opposes these pretended experiments; for she is greatly superior to the
mean idea of her entertained by any one who
puts his faith in them.   Similar outbursts, which
culminate in the hurling of an accusation of bad
faith at Newton (whom he accuses of having
knowingly altered the results of certain experiments), have caused scandal and have been
judged with great severity.   But while making
allowance for whatever small element of passion
may be mingled with his criticisms, and without
attempting to excuse Hegel by recording how
in these criticisms and even in the violence of
his language, he was in accord with some of his
eminent contemporaries and chiefly with Goethe,

it is certain that, on the whole, his polemic, alike
in its justice and in its unjust exaggeration, is
simply the logical consequence of the philosophic
position which Hegel took up in relation to the
intellectualism of exact science.

In the philosophy of nature also, as in the
philosophy of history, Hegel never dared to declare
the empirical and positive method altogether
erroneous, so that it could be wholly replaced
by the speculative method.   For him, the
empirical sciences, by constructing their laws
and their concepts, come to meet (*entgegenarbeiten*)
the work of the philosopher, to whom they offer
the material ready and half elaborated; and
as we have seen, he recommended agreement
between physics and philosophy.   And declarations of the same sort have been repeated
by the disciples of Hegel, such as Michelet,
Rosenkranz, and Vera.   This last compares
physicists to the labourers and the philosopher
to the architect, and says that "*la physique
rassemble et prépare les matériaux, que la philosophie vient ensuite marquer de sa forme.*" But
these are phrases, inspired by much impertinence
towards physicists and in any case empty of all
content.   For in truth, we do one of two things:
either we think that the empirical method is

capable of positing some laws, some genera, some
concepts, in a word, some truths; and in that
case we cannot understand why the other laws,
genera, truths and concepts, and the whole system
of them, should not be attainable with the same
method.   For the activity, which posits the first
naturalistic concept, reveals in that act its capacity
for positing the others and the whole; just as in
poetry, it is the same activity and no other which
forms the first verse, and which completes the
whole poem.   Or else we think that the empirical
method is not capable of any truth, however small;
and in that case the speculative method not only
has no need of the other, but can draw from it
no assistance.   To make verbal concessions to
physics and to the empirical method, is mere
trifling, and satisfies nobody.   Hegel, in considering the exact sciences to be a semi-philosophy,
really denied them altogether and absorbed them
in philosophy; which thus assumed all their rights
and duties.   And having thus placed so great a
burden upon the shoulders of philosophy, he had
no longer any right to lighten it by trying to
place part of it again upon the empirical sciences,
which were henceforth for him annulled and non-
existent.   All the rights imply all the duties; it
was henceforth the business of philosophy, not

of empirical science, to prove and to justify the
existence of this or that particular fact of nature ;
to discover stars, physical forces, chemical bodies,
physiological elements, unknown species of animals
and vegetables. That poor devil Krug was (it
seems this must henceforth be admitted) simply
the spokesman of good sense, when he demanded
of the natural philosophy of Schelling that it
should deduce the moon with its characteristics,
or a rose, a horse, a dog, or even only the pen
with which he, Krug, was writing at that moment.
Hegel from first to last of his writings made fun
of him and represented him as a comical person,[1]
and perhaps he may have been so ; but this does
not prevent Hegel's reply to Krug's objection
from being embarrassed and ambiguous beneath
an appearance of careless ease. For Hegel
seemed to say on the one hand that things of
that kind, individual facts (and all facts are
individual), do not belong to philosophy ; and
on the other, that the deduction is quite possible,
but that science has far more urgent tasks on
hand than the deduction of Mr. Krug's pen.
And the illustrious Neapolitan philologist and
physician, Salvatore Tommasi, was also, like

---

[1] See an article of 1802, in *Werke*, xvi. 57-59 ; and cf. *Encyclopaedia*,
§ 250 *n.*

Krug, in the right, when he replied, not without annoyance, to the Hegelian De Meis, who was a persistent protagonist of some sort of speculative physiology and pathology, that he would be disposed to turn his attention to the method recommended, only when some sort of discovery in medicine had been made by means of it : for example, the direct cure of pneumonia.

The attempt to hold on to the coat-tails of the empirical sciences, after having dismissed them, has then no other meaning, as has been said above with regard to history (and the basis of the natural sciences is historical), than to prove that Hegel's thesis is false. It does not heal the false nor make it true. But the analogy does not end here. Hegel, despairing of ever being able altogether to rationalize history, as his idea of a philosophy of history demanded, ended by arbitrarily cutting away a part of historical fact, which seemed to him more embarrassing than the rest, and by consigning it to fiction. And he did the same for the natural sciences, in relation to many classes and species of natural facts, to an infinite number of the appearances of reality, and to what are called rare cases, exceptions, or extraordinary beings. His discovery is delicious : it is of the *impotence*

of Nature (*die Ohnmacht der Natur*), of her
weakness, her swoonings and faintings, during
the difficult task of achieving the rationality of
the concept! But in the realm of history we did
not allow ourselves to be persuaded to abandon
a part of the facts, for we had learned from Hegel
himself that fact is sacred. So here, in the realm
of nature, having learned from him that there is
reason in the world, we shall not consent to
believe that one part of reality is rebellious or
inert towards reason. And what has been called
the *impotence of nature*, is clearly nothing but
the impotence of the *philosophy of nature*, as
conceived by Schelling and Hegel, to keep faith
with its own programme.

IX

THE CONSTRUCTION OF THE FALSE SCIENCES AND THE APPLICATION OF THE DIALECTIC TO THE INDIVIDUAL AND TO THE EMPIRICAL

HEGEL might have posited the idea of a philosophy of history and of a philosophy of nature; he might have desired it, have inculcated and defended it, and have done nothing else. A programme may be announced, and then it may be resolved not to carry it out: a thing which often happens, especially when the programme is dangerous. There are not a few systems and books, which have never gone beyond introductions and preliminaries, even in contemporary literature, and in their number are some of those announced with the greatest boasting. It would almost be worth while making an instructive catalogue of them. But Hegel did not leave the

philosophy of history and the philosophy of nature
as ideas in the air ; he constructed both effectively.
In this passage to actualization, he had to force
himself to treat individual facts and empirical
concepts like particular philosophical concepts ;
and since he had already applied the dialectic to
these last, he was obliged to proceed to the
*dialectic treatment of individual facts and of
empirical concepts.*

And this is the *second great abuse* that Hegel
made of his dialectical discovery. In order to
reach this second abuse, and to place ourselves
in a position to give its exact formulation and
genesis, it was indispensable to pass through the
first, and to work out its manifold consequences.
For this second abuse, that is, the failure to
recognize the autonomy of history and of the
positive sciences, is in its turn a consequence of
some of these. Without following that path in
all its twists and turnings, we could not com-
prehend how Hegel could ever have arrived at
so strange a thought : but by following it, we
reach, not only a full comprehension of the fact,
but a kind of feeling of admiration for the ingenuity of that closely-knit web of errors, for the
method of that madness, as Polonius would have
said.

The second abuse is the most commonly known : and it has contributed more than anything else to bring the Hegelian philosophy into disrepute.   If certain parts of philosophy were injured by the first, the second injured or menaced historical studies and the positive sciences ; and both alike reacted energetically in their own defence.

But in this connexion, we must not neglect to make certain observations.   The acquired conviction of the error of the method which Hegel defended and strove to apply, has involved in a general condemnation all Hegel's books on the history of civilization and of art, of philosophy and of religion, and on the various mathematical disciplines.   If the method is erroneous (so the ingenuous reasoning runs) what value, or what guarantee can attach to the results ?   The books from beginning to end will be sophisticated science and history.   And for this reason, not only is the *philosophy of nature* never sought and consulted by students of natural phenomena, and some translators even omit it from their versions of the *Encyclopaedia* ; but even Hegel's treatises upon historical subjects have themselves been viewed with diffidence, almost with the fear of being stained by contact with them.   Now, those books are to be examined, like all books, both in their general execution and in their details; for Hegel could act and on many occasions did act in them, either against or independently of his programme. Goethe, in the same way, according to the best authorities, wished to adopt methods in optics altogether foreign to physics, which have drawn down upon him the unanimous reproval of specialists in that subject, and yet in other branches of natural science, such as botany and anatomy, he made true and proper discoveries.[1] Indeed, speaking in general, the value of Schelling's and of Hegel's and of their disciples' books on the philosophy of nature continually increases as we pass from the more abstract to the more concrete parts, from physics to physiology, from the so-called inorganic world to the organic; and the reason for this is clearly that the utility of the mathematical method decreases in the more concrete parts. In any case, if Hegel did not, as it appears, obtain important results, nor make original observations in the positive parts of his naturalistic treatises (such as we find in the works of

---

[1] See Helmholtz's two lectures, "Über Goethes naturwissenschaftliche Arbeiten," and "Goethes Vorahnungen kommender naturwissenschaftlicher Ideen" (in *Vorträge und Reden*), Braunschweig, 1896, i. 23-47, ii. 335-361.

Treviranus, of Oken, etc.)[1]; if the best that he offers is perhaps always in pyschology and anthropology, a subject in which he was more properly versed; in the treatment of history, on the other hand, he stands on a level with the greatest historians of the nineteenth century, although it was (partly thanks to him) the century of historical writing. In the history of philosophy (of which, as has already been noted, he may be considered almost the creator) his observations are as full of truth as they are original. This applies to his characterizations of the Presocratics (and particularly of Parmenides, Heraclitus and of the Sophists), of Socrates himself, of Plato, of Aristotle, of the Stoics and of the Sceptics, of the Neo-Platonists and of Christianity; and in modern times, of the English empirical philosophy, of the critical-speculative period of Kant and of Schelling, of Jacobi and of the sentimentalists and mystics. In the study of ancient philosophy, he fully realized the profound difference between its way of presenting and of understanding problems and the way of modern philosophy; and the error of rendering its propositions in terms of current philosophy, as did Brucker or

---

[1] Compare with this, on the other hand, a note by Engels, *Antidühring*[3], pp. xv-xvi, which places in relief certain merits of Hegel as a physicist and naturalist.

Tiedmann.   His political history gives broad and
luminous views on the character and the connexions of the great historical epochs, of Greece,
of Rome, of the Middle Ages, of the Reformation
and of the French Revolution.   The history of
literature and of the arts, interspersed in his
lectures on æsthetics, contains views and judgments (for example, on the Homeric epos, on
ancient tragedy, on the Shakespearean drama, on
Italian painting of the Renaissance and on Dutch
painting), which have all become popular.   And
in truth, any one who makes a special study of
the historical ideas which were in vogue in the
nineteenth century and have become part of the
patrimony of our culture, would be astonished at
the great number of them which derive from
Hegel as their first source, or which received
definite form at his hands, although they have
been repeated and popularized by writers (like
Taine) who either did not know, or were in
error about their origin.   Again, it would be an
unfair criticism, though often made, to accuse
Hegel of historical errors, by making use of
researches and discoveries posterior to him.
(Sometimes these criticisms have rested on
doubtful discoveries, as when he has been blamed
for not having taken the "matriarchate" into

consideration, or for not having had a suspicion
of the sociological theories which assign the
origin of art to economic labour and industrial
decoration.)   No historian, however great, could
withstand such an examination : neither Thucy-
dides nor Polybius, nor Machiavelli, not even a
Niebuhr or a Mommsen.   And equally it would
be unfair to make too heavy and personal a charge
of certain political and national prejudices, which
appear neither more nor less frequently in his
constructions of history than in so many other
historians, philosophers and publicists : from the
Italian "primacy" of Gioberti to the contemporary Germanist manias of Herr Chamberlain
or of Herr Woltmann.

And in discussing these historical errors, which
were the consequence of philosophical errors, it
is necessary also to distinguish between those
arising from erroneous philosophical concepts
and those which are connected with his dialectic.
The former, Hegel often has in common with
other philosophers or with the philosophy of
his time (for example, the treatment of the history
of poetry and of art, based upon the concept of
an art that should be substantially religion or
philosophy ; and also, in general, the claim to
construct or to reconstruct speculatively the

course of history); but it is the latter which alone it concerns us to seek here.

But when all these reservations have been made, it is certain that we do meet in the books of Hegel examples of the dialectic treatment of the individual and empirical; and that suffices to explain and in part to justify the violent reaction of historians and naturalists against the dialectic itself.

For the reasons already given, there are fewer examples in his historical expositions; indeed, the history of philosophy may be considered almost altogether exempt. But the universal history which Hegel developed, is conceived in triadic form, as the Oriental world, the classical world and the Germanic world. These are thesis, antithesis, and synthesis, which receive concreteness for better or worse in the formula, that the Orient knew and knows *that only one man is free*; the Graeco-Roman world, that *some are free*; the Germanic world, that *all are free*. Hence the character of the first is despotism, of the second democracy and aristocracy, of the third monarchy. In order to establish this triad, Hegel is obliged to suppress many facts in space and time. In space, he altogether eliminates the fifth part of the world. Australia and the

other islands between Asia and America, seem
to him to be affected with "physical immaturity."
America itself is for him nothing but an append-
age of European civilization, and he refuses to
take into consideration the very ancient civiliza-
tions of Mexico and of Peru, because from what
we know of them, "they were altogether natural
and bound to perish at the approach of Spirit."
As regards time, he maintains that history only
begins when there are historians, hence the
German word *Geschichte* (or the Italian word
"storia") means both history *a parte subjecti*
and history *a parte objecti*. Peoples may have
passed a long life without a State; but this,
which is their *prehistory*, has nothing to do with
history. It was with reference to such limitations
in time and space that Hegel put down in one
of his note-books in the last year of his life: "In
universal history, the same division is valid as
was in use among the Greeks:—Greeks and
barbarians."[1] In this way, he sought to adapt
to his dialectic universal history as it appears in
the books of the historians; and he deluded
himself that he had found in the individual a
point of departure which should have the pre-
cision of the first term of the dialectic triad.

[1] *Aphorism, a. d. Berliner Periode*, in Rosenkranz, p. 559.

Such would be the spiritual Orient, where rises
the sun of history. But the triad, conquered
with such difficulty, totters at every particular
development which Hegel attempts. Indeed,
to take only those which first catch the eye, this
fundamental triad widens into a quatriad, the
Oriental world, the Greek world, the Roman
world, and the Germanic world; and in the
Orient, China and India are at once sacrificed
to Persia, which is for Hegel the first truly
historical nation. In like manner, the history
of art gives rise to a triad of Oriental or
Symbolical, Greek or Classical, and Christian
or Romantic, art : a triad whose very formulation
is unstable enough, deduced as it is from the
lack of equilibrium between content and form,
and of which the synthesis would be, not the
third term, but the second. Hegel seems also
to refer to a fourth artistic period, later than
the Romantic : and this would change this triad
also into a quatriad ; unless indeed the last phase
is meant to be the dissolution of art into philosophy. The history of religions is arranged
in three phases : natural religion, the religion of
the duplication of consciousness in itself, and the
religion of the transition to the religion of liberty.
The two last are also determined triadically : the

religion of reduplication into the religions of measure (the Chinese), of fancy (the Indian), and of internality (the Buddhist); the religion of the transition into the religions of nature, of spiritual liberty, and of absoluteness or absolute religion. And these are subdivided into new triads. The religion of nature is subdivided into the religions of light (the Persian), of pain (the Syrian), of the enigma (the Egyptian); the religion of spiritual liberty, into the religions of sublimity (the Jewish), of beauty (the Greek), of the intellect or of finality (the Roman). Absolute religion would then be Christianity. But one of the most curious examples of the dialectic construction of the individual is furnished by the characterization of the three parts of the world. Hegel, as has been said, got rid of the two others by saying that they did not seem to him mature, either physically or spiritually : the " new world," according to him, presented an incompletely developed division into a northern part and a southern part, in the manner of the magnet! But the ancient world exhibited the complete division into three parts; of which the first, Africa (the region of metal, of the lunar element, hardened by heat, in which man is confined within himself and obtuse), is mute spirit, which does not attain to knowledge; the second, Asia, is splendid bacchantic dissipation, the region of formless and indeterminate generation, which cannot order itself; and the third, Europe, represents consciousness, and constitutes the rational part of the earth, with its equilibrium of rivers, valleys, and mountains; and the centre of Europe is Germany.[1]

The dialectic construction runs riot in the philosophy of nature, the field of the empirical concepts. In its positive part, that book is at bottom nothing but a compendium of mathematical and naturalistic disciplines, divided into three sections: first, geometry and mechanics, second, astronomy, physics and chemistry; third, mineralogy, botany, zoology, geology and physiology. This compendium of different sorts of knowledge is arranged in the fundamental triad of mechanics, physics and organic physics and the whole is subdivided into minor triads. We need not concern ourselves with the idea that since in universal history the point of convergence and the final result is the Germanic spirit, so in the cosmological conception of Hegel, the centre of the universe is the Earth (and Germany would be the centre of the earth, at least according to the words above quoted).

[1] *Naturphilosophie*, § 340 Zus.

This only shows once more how a lofty philosophical intellect can now and then be subjugated by sentiment and prejudice. Let us rather consider some examples of the dialectic of geometry and of physics. Besides the three dimensions of space, Hegel posits three dimensions of time; past, present, and future; but whereas he observes that the three dimensions of time are not existentially differentiated in nature, he seems to admit that the three dimensions of space are so differentiated. In any case, these three would be founded upon the nature of the concept, although (he says) the determinations of the concept, in this first form of externality, abstract quantity, are only superficial and constitute differences which are altogether empty. They are superficial, they are empty, they are arbitrary; yet Hegel deduces them dialectically. The point is the negation of space; but it is a negation essentially spatial; and so becomes a line; and the negation of the negation is the surface! And he offers the deduction of the celestial bodies; the central body is the thesis, the moon and the comets are the bodies of the antithesis; the synthesis, the body of the concrete totality, is the planet. Magnetism seems to him the demonstration *ad oculos* of the dialectic concept in nature, of the complete syllogism. The two poles are the extremities of a real line existing in sense, yet they do not possess sensible and mechanical reality, but ideal reality, and shew themselves to be altogether inseparable. The point of in-difference, in which their substance finds place, is their unity as determinations of the concept, in such a way that they receive sense and exist-ence only in such a unity ; and polarity is only the relation of such moments. Owing to the necessity of the dialectic form, Hegel combats the identification of magnetism, electricity, and chemistry, which physical science tries to effect ; and wishes the three facts to be both united and distinct. He would be equally opposed to the physiologists, who abolish the clear distinction between the animal cell and the vegetable cell, or consider life as disseminated everywhere. The three "natural kingdoms" answered his triadic theory too well to permit of his not preserving them in dialectic form, as geological, vegetable and animal nature. In the first, life posits to itself its own conditions ; in the second, the individual is still external to its own members, which are themselves individuals ; in the third, the members exist essentially as members of the

individual, and therefore the individual is subject.
The dialectic applies also each of these forms of
nature : the process of the plant is divided into
three syllogisms, that is to say, into the process
of formation, into the process of opposition toward
inorganic nature, and into the process of reproduction, the unity of the two preceding. The dialectical reconstruction of the five senses, which
are five and not three, is more laborious. But
Hegel is not dismayed. For him the senses are
five, yet they are three. The first is that which
belongs to the mechanical sphere, of weight and
cohesion and of their change, that is to say, the
sense of touch. The second is—the two senses
of the antithesis, that is to say that of particularized aerity, and that which comprehends the
neutrality of concrete water, and the antithesis
of the solution of concrete neutrality : taste and
smell. The third is the sense of ideality, and it
also is double : that is to say, the sense of ideality
as manifestation of the external by the external,
of light in general, and more precisely, of light
determined in the concrete externality of colour ;
and the sense of the manifestation of internality,
which makes itself known as such in its ex-
ternalization, by tone ; that is to say, sight and
hearing !

Other examples of this dialectic of the empirical are to be found in profusion in what for us is also a philosophy of nature (in the gnoseological sense), or a philosophy of the empirical; *i.e.* in many parts of the æsthetic, of the logic, and of the philosophy of spirit.   In the æsthetic, the system of the arts is developed triadically.   The first of the arts, architecture, creates the temple of God : the second, sculpture, creates God himself; the˙third expresses the feelings of the faithful in colours, tones, and words, and is subdivided into painting, music, and poetry.   The labour of condensing into three, what empirically is determined by another number (the five arts into three, the five senses into three) is spared to him in the fields of poetry and of rhetoric, in which he found ready the tripartition into lyric, epic, and dramatic poetry, as in natural science he found the three natural kingdoms.   In logic, his classification of the judgments is, with a new terminology, word for word the same as that of Kant, which has a quatriad as basis : the judgment of quality becomes that of existence, the judgment of quantity that of reflexion, the judgment of relation that of necessity, the judgment of modality that of the concept ; and the triadic subdivisions of these are preserved.   The syl-

logism (which is the synthesis in relation to
judgment as antithesis, or the restoration of the
concept in the judgment and so the unity and
truth of both, is also developed triadically, as
syllogism of determinate being, syllogism of
reflexion, and syllogism of necessity.   In the
philosophy of spirit, Hegel knows well that
psychology cannot serve as basis for philosophy ;
yet he treats it dialectically.   Subjective spirit is
developed in the three degrees of anthropology,
of phenomenology and of psychology ; the first
includes the soul, natural, sentient, and real ; the
second, consciousness, consciousness of self, and
reason ; the third, theoretic, practical, and free
spirit.   Objective spirit has the three moments
of rights, morality, and ethics : rights are subdivided into rights of property, of contract, and
of rights against wrong.   The ethical sphere is
subdivided into family, civil society, and the
State ; the State, finally, into internal rights,
external rights, and (a curious leap) universal
history.

The Hegelian dialectic has so often been
satirized, but no satire can compare with that
which the author himself unconsciously gives
of it, when he tries to think Africa, Asia, and
Europe, or the hand, the nose, and the ear, or

family patrimony, paternal authority, and the last
will and testament, with the same rhythm with
which he had thought being, nothing, and becoming. It sometimes seems as if Hegel was not
in full possession of his thought, so much so that
he was obliged to assist himself with mythology :
in the same way that (according to an ingenious
interpretation of Hegel himself) Plato, when his
thought failed to master certain arduous problems
which in his time were not yet ripe for solution,
replaced the solution by thought with the solution by imagination, the concept with the myth.

X

DUALISM NOT OVERCOME

THE panlogism, which has been noted in the system of Hegel, is nothing but the sum of the errors arising from the misuse of the dialectic, which I have analyzed and exposed one by one. It is the substitution of philosophic thought for all the other processes of the spirit, which must all acquire logical (philosophical) form and perish. But it is an error to consider panlogism as the fundamental characteristic of the system, when it is but a morbid excrescence, growing from it. There is no need to adduce as proof of Hegel's panlogism his identification of logic and metaphysic, in that for him logic is at the same time metaphysic. Because for Hegel *Logic*, so-called, had nothing in common with the logic of the schools (nor, in general, with a science of logic as a particular philosophical science). His logic was the doctrine of the categories, of which logic, in the narrow sense, constituted only one, or only one group. And since the categories embraced all spirit and all reality, it is clear that the identification of logic and metaphysic, of logic and philosophy, was at bottom nothing more than the identification of metaphysic with metaphysic, of philosophy with philosophy. That his meta-physic and philosophy are developed, in part, as panlogism, is true; but it is a different question. The error lies exactly in the use of the principle, not in the principle by itself.

The other accusation which has been made against the system of Hegel, that it is a more or less masked dualism, would appear to be irreconcilable with the accusation of panlogism; but it is not so. Since error can never affirm itself with the full coherence of truth, the error of panlogism converts itself into its contrary, that is, into dualism. The field of this conversion is the philosophy of nature, where, as has been shown, there appears everywhere, solid and persistent, the old concept of nature, suggested by the physical and natural sciences. Hegel gave this concept a philosophical value, thereby making it the thought of a reality which should stand opposed to, or behind, the reality of spirit. The critical point of this conversion,

or the revelation of the dualism, which is discovered at the very moment when he tries to
conceal it, is the celebrated transition from the
idea to nature, on which Hegel expressed himself very briefly and obscurely, and on which
his disciples have shed so many words, but so
little light: " The idea, which is for itself, considered according to this unity with itself, is
intuitive.   But, as intuition, the idea is brought
into the one-sided determination of immediacy
or negation, by means of extrinsic reflexion.
The absolute freedom of the idea is therefore
that it does not pass only into life, nor allow
life to appear in it only as finite knowledge; but
in the absolute truth of itself, it resolves to allow
to go freely out of itself, as nature, the moment of
its particularity or of its first determination and
of its otherness, the immediate idea which is its
reflexion " (*Enc.* par. 244).

This conversion and this transition are so
dangerous, that many interpretations of the
Hegelian thought have been proposed (and
others might be proposed) in order to avoid the
danger, to eliminate the dualism and to preserve to the system its initial motive, which is
absolute idealism, or substance as subject.   But
none of those interpretations seems to be in

accordance with the genuine thought of the philosopher.

Thus it may be convenient to maintain that the transition from the idea to nature is, for Hegel, nothing but the transition from philosophy to experience, from philosophy to natural science, whose existence, subsistence, and independence side by side with philosophy, Hegel would never have thought of denying. The system of Hegel would become in this way a philosophy of mind or of spirit, universal, extraneous, but not hostile to experience, that is, to the observation and study of particular historical and natural facts. But such an interpretation is met by the simple consideration, that Hegel does not pass from philosophy to natural (empirical) *science*, but from logic or philosophy in general to the *philosophy* of nature ; and therefore he understands nature, not as the empirical concept in contrast with the speculative, but as a speculative concept, which has equal rights with every other.

This same difficulty confronts the interpretation which declares that there is no transition, either logical or temporal, between the idea and nature, because the idea does not *become* nature, but is already nature ; the individual is the universal, and the universal is the individual.

Doubtless, in this way dualism would be avoided ;
because it is the universal alone which is grasped
in philosophical consideration. The individual
(which, philosophically, is the universal itself) is
realized, in so far as it is merely individual, by intuition, that is to say, by a level of spirit, which pre-
cedes the philosophical level and is its condition.
But Hegel has not abandoned the individual to
the poets or historians : he thought the philosophy
of the individual, when he thought the philosophy
of nature and of history. In order to interpret
him in the manner proposed, it would be necessary to cut out from his system, not some few
incidental pages of digression, but to mutilate
it by whole books and sections, and these from
among the parts, which, to the author at least,
seemed to be vital organs of the whole structure.

A third interpretation could be elaborated,
founded upon a meaning of the word "nature,"
of which there are traces in Hegel, as the negative
moment of spirit, as passivity opposed to activity,
the mechanical opposed to the teleological, as not-
being opposed to being. In this case, spirit and
nature would not be two distinct concepts, concepts
of two realities, or of two forms of reality ; but
one unique concept of the unique reality, which
is synthesis of opposites, dialectic and develop-

ment ; and its unity would be saved. The idea, which is alienated from itself as nature, to return to itself in spirit, would be spirit itself, understood in its concreteness, which includes the negative moment. The Italian thinker, Spaventa, came very near this interpretation, when he wrote that : " the logos in itself is not reality, save in so far as it is Logic, that is, spirit as thought of thought (pure thought) ; and nature, *fixed* as nature, is not self-sufficient, and therefore it not only pre-supposes ideally the logos, but has absolute spirit as its real principle, precisely because it has it as its real and absolute end."[1] Yet, side by side with this meaning of the word nature as negation and not-being (as side by side with the meaning of the word nature as the individual and the matter of intuition), Hegel maintains the idea of nature understood as reality, as the other of spirit, τὸ ἕτερον καθ' αὑτό (*the other in itself*). Indeed, were this not so, Hegel could never have thought of constructing a philosophy of the negative, of not being, of what is a mere abstraction ; whereas he does write a philosophy of nature, and there-fore understands by the object of that philosophy something positive.

Finally, some have attempted to interpret the

---

[1] *Principî di etica*, pp. 53-54.

Hegelian tripartition of logos, nature and spirit,
as if nature and spirit were nothing but the
concrete spirit itself, divided only empirically into
two parts; and the logos would signify the true
reality that constitutes both, their identity in the
apparent division: it would be spirit in its universality, and not only as it appears in the world
called social or human, when that is empirically separated from the rest.   But it would be
impossible to cancel the profound distinction
which Hegel makes between nature and spirit,
and which he affirms as the distinction between
an unconscious and a conscious logicity.   Pan-
psychism was far from Hegel's intention; for him,
thought belonged to man and was foreign to the
animal; in nature, there is not *thought*, but only
determinations of thought, which is different;
there certainly is an intelligence, but, as Schelling
said (and Hegel approved), it is intelligence petri-
fied.   Therefore Hegel maintained that in nature
the forms of spirit are not, as in the conscious
spirit, resolved into one another, but have the
position of separate existences.   Matter and
movement, for example, exist as facts in the solar
system; the determinations of the senses exist
as a quality of bodies, and also separately, as
elements, and so on (*Enc.* par. 380): the dialectic

nature of the concept stands as a natural fact, in the positive and negative poles of the magnet. To regard nature and spirit as a single series, distinguishable into two only by a convention, as civilized man is distinguished from the savage, may be a just conception ; but it was altogether foreign to the intention of Hegel.   His distinction of nature and spirit, whatever may be said to the contrary, is qualitative ; if the difference between unconscious and conscious beings, between things and thinkers, is qualitative.

In the genuine thought of Hegel, as found in his philosophy of nature, spirit and nature are, then, two realities : the one opposed to the other, or the one the basis of the other, but, in any case, each distinct from the other.   Therefore he had recourse to a third term, the logos : the necessity of overcoming the dualism drove him to try to overcome it with the triadic form, which had done such excellent service in overcoming the dualism of opposites.   But since nature and spirit are not opposites in his thought, they are not two abstractions, but two concrete realities ; and the triadic form was inapplicable.   Nor was it valid to apply the form of criticism which, also with marvellous results, he had adopted for the concepts of reflexion, in the doctrine of the essence ;

since, for him, nature and spirit, in the sense in
which he took them, were not concepts of reflexion, difficult to distinguish, but two quite distinct concepts, of quite determinate character. The
third term, the Logos, is, in his triad, the first,
the thesis. But, while the content of the second
term, the antithesis, is clearly nothing but the
whole of mathematical, physical, and natural
theories; and the content of the third term, the
synthesis, is, equally clearly, psychology on the
one hand, and on the other, the philosophies of
rights, of art, of religion, and of the absolute
spirit or Idea; the first, the thesis, the Logos,
has no content of its own, but borrows it from
the other two parts, especially from the last, and
mingles with it a polemic against inadequate
philosophies. The fact is, that this Logos, for
him who truly separates it from nature and from
spirit and looks it well in the face, reveals itself
as nothing but the dark foundation of the old
metaphysic: God, in whom were united the two
substances of Descartes, the *substantia sive Deus*,
which, in Spinoza, supported the two attributes
of thought and of extension. It is the Absolute
of Schelling, indifference of nature and of spirit;
or the blind (but not too blind) Will of Schopenhauer, from which come forth nature and

consciousness; or the Unconscious of Edward von Hartmann, which, also with much manifestation of reason, gives a beginning to consciousness. Hegel had reproached Schelling with conceiving the Absolute as substance and not as subject. But his Logos is indeed a subject, which cannot be thought as subject, or rather, which cannot be thought at all. It is, as Hegel himself says, "God in his eternal essence before the creation of nature and of the finite spirit"; and we can well think God in nature and in the finite spirit, *Deus in nobis et nos*, but certainly not a God *outside* or *prior* to nature and man. The triadic expedient, and the term Logos, to which Hegel has recourse, show that he is always entangled in dualism; that he struggles valiantly against it, but does not escape from it.

This *dualism not overcome*, in which Hegel's absolute idealism becomes entangled, owing to the grave logical error he has committed, is the reason of the division of the Hegelian school into a right and a left, and for the eventual extension of the latter to an extreme left. The right wing interpreted Hegel theistically. The subject, the Logos of Hegel, was the personal God; and the relation of the Hegelian philosophy to Christianity was not exhausted in the recognition of the great philosophical element contained in Christian theology, but extended to a much more substantial agreement. The left wing was opposed to all transcendence and to the whole conception of a personal God. It emphasized the character of immanence of the system, and finally came to sympathize with philosophic materialism, in so far as this in its own way has an immanent and not a transcendental character. It would be impossible to decide which of the two interpretations was the more faithful to the thought of Hegel; for both of them were founded upon Hegelian doctrines, and were opposed and hostile to one another, precisely because those doctrines were contradictory.

XI

THE CRITICISM AND CONTINUATION
OF THE THOUGHT OF HEGEL

CONCLUSION

WITH the interpretation of the philosophy of
Hegel, which I have attempted in this essay,
I have declared at the same time what, in my
opinion, is the task that should fall to its critics
and to those who continue it. It was necessary
to preserve the vital part of it, that is to say,
the new concept of the concept, the concrete
universal, together with the dialectic of opposites
and the doctrine of degrees of reality; to refute
with the help of that new concept and by developing it, all panlogism, and every speculative construction of the individual and of the empirical, of
history and of nature; to recognize the autonomy
of the various forms of spirit, while preserving
their necessary connexion and unity; and finally,
to resolve the whole philosophy into a *pure philo-*

sophy of spirit (or a logic-metaphysic, as it might then have been called). It was necessary to draw forth the Hegelian thought "from the sheath of its members," that is to say, of its false members, which had been badly attached to it; and to permit it to form its own members, answering to the nature of the primitive germ.

The school of Hegel failed altogether in this task. It divided, as has been observed, into right and left, and subdivided into secondary fractions, on the importance to be attached to the respective tendencies towards transcendence and towards immanence, in the system; and yet it remained wholly united in preserving and increasing the dialectical entanglement, the confusion between the dialectic of opposites and the dialectic of distincts, between the dialectic of the absolute and the dialectic of the contingent. Michelet, for example, the editor of the *Philosophy of Nature*, amused himself with dialectically correcting certain details; such as the place that belongs to the fifth part of the world in the dialectic of geography, which we have already mentioned. He believed that the islands of Oceania represent the ultimate future of the human race, the extreme development of democratic *self-government*. And to those who did not see clearly into dia-

lectic modes of reasoning, Michelet replied that
the dialectic method, like artistic creation, makes
no claim to universal acceptance, but must remain
"a specific talent of the favourite of the Gods."
Truly this was far from doing honour to the
master, who had affirmed so persistently and with
so profoundly human a sense, that philosophy
must not be esoteric, but exoteric. Rosenkranz
(another of the principal representatives of the
right wing), after he had constructed in his
Æsthetic of the Ugly, in a way which I shall
content myself with calling bizarre, all the terms
of the coarsest and most vulgar psychology, also
proposed re-arrangements and corrections of the
philosophy of nature. His corrections concerned,
e.g. the dignity of the fixed stars, which Hegel
was supposed to have slighted in favour of the
planets and of the earth ; the division between
physics and astronomy, which Hegel was supposed
to have wrongfully confused ; the transference of
the process of crystallization from the physical to
the organic ; and the like. But on the other
hand, he never abandoned the Hegelian assumption of the philosophy of nature ; indeed, where
Hegel had lighted on a glimpse of the truth by
declaring the impossibility of a dialectic construction of mathematics, Rosenkranz was ready

to contradict him. " This cannot be admitted,"
he exclaims, " because if the dialectic method be
universal, why should mathematics be excluded
from it ? " Vera, the Italian champion of ortho-
doxy, continued the exploits against Newton.
He maintained that the science of nature is to
be effected by three methods, the experimental,
the mathematical, and the speculative, which last
is the crown of the three : and he wrote, among
other things : " *Nous disons qu'il y a un air, une
lumière, et même un temps et un espace apparents
et qui sont sentis, et un air, une lumière, etc., qui
n'apparaissent point et qui sont simplement pensés.*"

Passing from the extreme right to the extreme
left, and dwelling for a moment upon a writer,
who has in recent times been much known and
discussed in Italy, Frederick Engels (the friend
and collaborator of Karl Marx), we can see how
he reduced philosophy, by equating it to the
positive sciences, and preserving of it only " the
doctrine of thought and of its laws : formal (!)
logic and the dialectic." And of this dialectic,
" which was nothing but the science of the
general laws of the movement and development
of human societies and of thought," Engels
gave such examples as the following. A grain
of barley, put into the earth, sprouts, and becom-

ing a plant, is negated; but other grains come from the plant : and this is the negation of the negation. The chrysalis is negated when the butterfly comes out of it; but the butterfly reproduces the chrysalis—again the negation of the negation. In arithmetic, a is negated by $-a$, but, negating the negation, we have $-a \times -a = a^2$; that is to say, the first a raised to a power. In history, civilization begins with common proprietorship of the soil; private property denies primitive communism; socialism will effect the negation of the negation, reproducing the primitive communism, but raised to a higher power. In the history of philosophy, the first moment is original materialism; this is negated by idealism, which afterwards suffers the negation of its negation, in dialectical materialism. Nor can it be objected (added Engels), that it is possible to negate a grain of barley by eating it, or an insect by treading upon it, or the positive magnitude a by cancelling it; because the negation must be such as to render possible the negation of the negation : otherwise (he remarks ingenuously), there would not be a dialectic process.[1]

---

[1] *Antidühring*, intr., pp. 9-11, and on the negation of the negation, pp. 137-146. This extract is also to be found in Italian in the Appendix of Labriola's book, *Discorrendo di Socialismo e di filosofia* (Rome, 1897), pp. 168-178.

Who will narrate in all their wealth of amusing details the lamentable fortunes of the dialectic method at the hands of Hegel's disciples? One of them dialecticized spirit as the masculine principle, nature as the feminine, and history as the matrimonial union. Another found in the Oriental world, the category of being; in the classical world, the category of essence; and in the modern world, the category of the concept. For yet another, antiquity was the kingdom of art; the modern world, that of philosophy; the future was to be the kingdom of morality; and in the ancient world, Athens was made to correspond with dynamic electricity, Sparta with static electricity, Macedonia with electro-magnetism, Persia with light, Rome with expansive and absorbent heat.[1] These stupidities are to be found in profusion in books *illustrium virorum* as well as *obscurorum*; nor can it be said that those of the obscure men are the least significant.

The best of the school were those who, feeling themselves unable to go beyond Hegel, or believing that the time was not yet ripe for doing so, limited themselves to preserving the doctrines of

---

[1] These examples are taken from C. Knapp, from A. v. Cieszkowski, etc., in P. Barth, *Geschichtsphilosophie Hegels u. d. Hegelianer*, pp. 29, 62. For other characteristic examples, see the historical part of my *Æsthetic*, c. 13.

the master as a sacred trust, emphasizing the profound elements of truth in them, and refraining, as though through an instinct for the truth, from insisting upon the difficult parts (the philosophy of nature, or the philosophy of history), yet without refuting them explicitly. They showed their cautious and critical spirit, also, in, as it were, reconducting Hegel to his Kantian foundations, and in making the necessity of the transition from Kant to Hegel the object of their continuous study. Such were Kuno Fischer in Germany, to whom we owe a lucid re-elaboration of the Hegelian logic;[1] Bertrando Spaventa in Italy; Stirling in Great Britain;[2] and several of the students whom they formed in the three countries. Spaventa did not pass beyond or transform Hegel, but he foresaw clearly that this was necessary and had to happen. "In the philosophers (he remarked on this subject), in the true philosophers, there is always something underneath, which is more than they themselves and of which they are not conscious; and this is

---

[1] See his *Logik und Metaphysik* (1852), especially in the second edition of 1865.

[2] J. Stirling, *The Secret of Hegel* (London, 1865): "*That secret may be indicated at shortest thus : as Aristotle—with considerable assistance from Plato—made explicit the abstract universal, that was implicit in Socrates, so Hegel—with less considerable assistance from Fichte and Schelling—made explicit the concrete universal, that was implicit in Kant*" (i. p. 11 ; cf. p. 317).

the germ of a new life. To repeat the philosophers mechanically, is to suffocate this germ,
to impede its developing and becoming a new
and more perfect system." [1]

Of the adversaries of Hegel, it must be said
that they too failed of their duty; and indeed,
had they done it, they would not have been the
adversaries, but the disciples and continuers of
his thought. For if his fanatical followers preserved the dialectic, just as it stood, with its
confusions and false applications, they, on the
other hand, rejected it altogether; thus falling
into an analogous but opposite error. We may
set aside the bizarre Schopenhauer, who belched
forth contumelies against Hegel, but spoke of
him by hearsay, without knowing anything precise about him. [2] Indeed his calumnious gossip
never rises above the level of the general or
anecdotic. Herbart, far better balanced, at least
recognized in Hegel " one of those rare men born
for speculation"; and held that the Hegelian
philosophy, because of the clear relief in which
it sets the contradictions, with which reality, as it
presents itself to thought, is charged, constitutes

---

[1] Proluzione e introduzione cit., pp. 182-183.

[2] Such is also the opinion of the anti-Hegelian R. Haym, in his essay
on Schopenhauer (reprinted in the *Gesammelte Aufsätze*, Berlin, 1903);
cf. pp. 330-31.

the best propaedeutic to metaphysic.[1] But if we read the refutations of the dialectic by Trendelenburg in Germany, by Rosmini in Italy, by Janet in France (to name only the most important), we cannot but experience a feeling of distrust; for when we realize that a critic makes his task too easy, we divine from his very words of condemnation and of depreciation that there is something much more profound in the question, which he has failed to reach. Doubtless those ingenious confuters brought to light difficulties, and sometimes errors; but they did not show the true genesis of the errors, how they derived from the exaggeration of a new and great truth. "To confute a philosophy (Hegel himself said) means nothing but to surpass its limits, and to lower its determinate principle, so as to make of it an ideal moment."[2]

But with the new generation that reached maturity after 1848, the philosophical adversaries of Hegel were soon succeeded by barbaric adversaries. These hated nothing in Hegel but philosophy itself, which he represented in all its grandiose severity : Philosophy, which is without heart and without compassion for the feeble-

[1] See his criticism of the *Encyclopaedia*, *Werke*, ed. Hartenstein, xii. 670, 685.

[2] *Enc.* § 86 *Zus.*

minded and for the lazy: Philosophy, which is not to be placated with the specious offerings of sentiment and of fancy, nor with the light foods of half-science. For these, Hegel was the un-avenged shade of the speculative need of the human spirit; a shade which seemed disposed to take its own revenge at any moment. Hence the fierce hatred of Hegel: a hatred composed of fear and of remorse, and certainly not caused by the errors of his system. Hegel had observed that after Fichte philosophy had become too subtle, and could no longer be an occupation for the *beau monde* and for the cultured public, as it had been in the eighteenth century, previous to Kant.[1] But the positivist regression reduced minds to such an extremity, that they were rendered blind to the distinction between the concept and sensation, between speculation and empiricism. How then could it have been possible for such an age, which lacked all the elementary or propaedeutic distinctions, to understand or criticize Hegel, who assumes the knowledge and solution of the elementary problems, whose thought revolves round the ultimate and most refined questions, who breathes and lives on the most lofty summits? For such as these, to look

[1] *Gesch. d. Phil.*[2], iii. 577-8.

upon him was to awake in themselves the sad
consciousness of impotence, with its agitations
and irritations, and its ferocious condemnation
of joys that it may not taste.

Happily, in our day, there is an improvement
in our intellectual outlook. It is more favourable
to philosophy in general, and more favourable to
Hegel himself. We are now beginning to possess
a philosophy of art and of language, a theory of
history, a gnoseology of the mathematical and
naturalistic disciplines, which render impossible
the reappearance of those errors, in which Hegel
became entangled. In particular, the old concept
of nature, inherited from science, or rather from
the philosophy of the seventeenth century, is
in process of dissolution : every day it becomes
clearer how nature, as a concept, is a product of
the practical activity of man ; and it is only when
he forgets how he has acquired it, that he finds
it opposed to him as something external, which
terrifies him with its aspect of impenetrable
mystery. On the other hand, a certain philosophical romanticism is everywhere appearing
again, and this is a condition (though nothing
more than a condition) for the true understanding
of Hegel and all the philosophers of his time.
People are sighing again for mysticism and for

immediate knowledge, after the manner of Jacobi ;
and they are setting up again the old Schellinghian
ideal of an æsthetic contemplation, which should
give to the spirit a thirst for truth and for concreteness, something that (natural) science cannot
give. Thus, Bergson, one of the writers who
have attached themselves to this movement,
advocates as a metaphysic of the absolute, an
intuitive knowledge, "*qui s'installe dans le mouve-
ment et adopte la vie même des choses.*" [1]   But was
not this just what Hegel demanded, and the
point from which he began—to find a form of
mind, which should be mobile as the movement
of the real, which should participate in the life of
things, which should feel "the pulse of reality,"
and should mentally reproduce the rhythm of its
development, without breaking it into pieces or
making it rigid and falsifying it ?

But for Hegel, such a view was only a starting-
point, not a conclusion, as it is for the writer we
have quoted, and for others of like tendencies.
The renunciation of thought would have been
asked of Hegel in vain. And to have shown
that the demand of concrete knowledge is satisfied
in the form of thought, is his great merit, his

---

[1] " Introduction à la Métaphysique " in *Revue de métaph. et de morale,*
xi. p. 29.

immortal discovery. Hence the necessity of studying Hegel critically, and of sifting the intimate and vital elements of his thought from the extrinsic and dead. The modern consciousness can neither accept the whole of Hegel, nor wholly refute him, as used to be done fifty years ago. In relation to him it stands in the position of the Roman poet to his lady : *nec tecum vivere possum, nec sine te.* It does not appear that we can now obtain this critical revision of Hegelianism from its German fatherland, which is so forgetful of its great son that it has not even reprinted his works and frequently expresses judgments concerning him, which astound us who belong to this remote fringe of Italy, for we have never altogether forgotten him, and have in some wise made him our own, uniting him in brotherhood with our Nolan Bruno and with our Vico, the Parthenopean. Far more important than the German studies, are the studies on Hegelianism, which have been carried on for over thirty years in England. There the work of Stirling has shown itself to be very fruitful ; for there Hegel is clearly expounded, truthfully interpreted and criticized reverently and with freedom of mind. In return, the powerful spirit of George Hegel has for the first time awakened to the speculative

life the minds of the English, who have been for
centuries the world purveyors of empirical philosophy and who even in the last century seemed
incapable of producing any philosophers better
than Stuart Mill and Herbert Spencer.

Now, if any one were to ask me if he should
or should not be an " Hegelian," and if I am an
Hegelian, I might, after all I have said, dispense
with a reply.   Yet I wish as a corollary, to answer
here this question in a way which is perhaps
derived from that very philosophy.   I am, and
believe it necessary to be, an Hegelian; but in
the same sense in which any one who has a philosophical spirit and philosophical culture in our
time, is and feels himself to be at once: *Eleatic,
Heraclitean, Socratic, Platonic, Aristotelian, Stoic,
Sceptic, Neoplatonic, Christian, Buddhist, Cartesian, Spinozist, Leibnizian, Vichian, Kantian;*
and so on.   That is to say, in the sense that no
thinker and no historical movement of thought
come to pass without bearing fruit, without
depositing an element of truth, which forms part,
consciously or no, of living modern thought.
Neither I nor any sensible person would wish to
be an Hegelian, in the sense of a servile and
obsequious follower, who professes to accept
every word of the master, or in the sense of a

religious sectarian, who considers disagreement
a sin. In short, Hegel too has discovered a
moment of the truth ; to this moment we must
accord recognition and value. That is all. If
this does not happen just at present, it does not
much matter. *The Idea is not in a hurry*, as
Hegel used to say. The same content of truth
must be reached, sooner or later, by a different
way ; and, if we have not availed ourselves of his
direct help, yet when we look back upon the
history of thought, we must still proclaim him,
with much marvel, a prophet.

But the first condition for resolving whether
to accept or to reject the doctrines which Hegel
propounds (I am constrained to make explicit
what I should have preferred to leave to be
understood) is to *read his books :* and to put an
end to the spectacle, half comical and half dis-
gusting, of the accusation and the abuse of a
philosopher by critics who do not know him, and
who wage a foolish war with a ridiculous puppet
created by their own imaginations, under the
ignoble sway of traditional prejudice and intellectual laziness.

THE END